ELIZABETHAN NEEDLEWORK
ACCESSORIES

The second title in the
Elizabethan Needlework series

BY SHEILA MARSHALL

Embroidery threads used throughout this book were supplied by
Warnaar Trading Company Limited.

Published by Georgeson Publishing Limited
P.O. Box 100-667, North Shore Mail Centre, Auckland, New Zealand.
Phone: 64 9 410 2079 Facsimile: 64 9 410 2069
E mail: gpl@georgeson.co.nz

ISBN 0 473 04977-5

First published June 1998, first reprint November 1998,
second reprint May 1999

Series Editor :   Pru Georgeson
Photography :   Maria Sainsbury
Layout and Illustrations :   Valancy Stevens

Printed in New Zealand

CONTENTS

INTRODUCTION

In this book we continue the Elizabethan journey which was begun in *Exploring Elizabethan Embroidery*. The projects are my interpretation of Elizabethan embroidery inspired by the richness of the work seen in London museums during my three years training at Art School.

I introduce new stitches and techniques giving different and creative ways to achieve a variety of textures, colours and effects that even 400 years later are pleasing to look at and fun to embroider. I have tried to balance the designs so that they are interesting and enjoyable to stitch as well as being effective and attractive. I always feel that this type of embroidery actually grows fairly quickly, despite the fact that the designs are 'busy'.

There has been an upsurge of interest in all forms of embroidery. Raised and Elizabethan embroidery is particularly appealing because of the three dimensional effect that colour and a variety of stitches can produce. Elizabethan style embroidery is truly a work of art.

It has been a great joy to me when teaching Elizabethan embroidery to see the pleasure and sense of accomplishment my students feel when they realise they can actually reproduce this rich and elaborate work which they had previously thought would be too difficult. I hope you too will gain this pleasure and satisfaction from my book.

Sheila Marshall, March 1998

How to Use this Book

This book, the second in our Elizabethan Needlework Series, has been written to continue exploration of the stitch techniques which have been so popular in *Exploring Elizabethan Embroidery*. In that book we introduced readers to the stitches and techniques used in Elizabethan Embroidery. In this book we build upon the knowledge gained in the first book and introduce further stitches and new techniques to enable you to develop your mastery of this most fascinating embroidery technique. All the stitches and techniques used in this book are covered in the 'Stitch Section' of the book.

Under necessities we cover different aspects of this embroidery from the needles to use, fabrics to stitch on and threads to experiment with. We also cover a variety of different methods of transferring designs, needed for the different materials stitched on. Increasing and decreasing the size of designs, backing fabrics ready for stitching and the use of frames is also covered.

The Stitch Section introduces in large, clear, easy-to-follow diagrams the different stitches and techniques used here. Even if these stitches are new to you, I am sure you will find our instructions make them all easy to master.

We then present seven different projects all tied in with the theme of the book *Elizabethan Needlework Accessories*. Embroiderers need a variety of different tools for their craft and here we present an attractive selection of some of the items an embroiderer needs! They have been worked on a variety of different materials, including silk, satins, velvet and linen to show just how versatile this technique is and how attractive it looks on a variety of different fabrics. You could make all the projects as individual pieces or make them as a set, matching colours and fabrics to create heirlooms for the future. It is your choice!

Each item of embroidery is shown in full colour in the central pages of this book. One page is devoted to each different project so that the photos can serve as an inspiration as well as a guide to you when stitching.

Our earlier publication *Exploring Elizabethan Embroidery*, has more beautiful flowers and different techniques and these flowers and techniques can be used with the techniques described here to widen your repertoire. In this book the individual flowers are on a smaller scale so just remember to adjust the size of the flowers from *Exploring Elizabethan Embroidery* to be the same size as the flowers given in the project you are working on from this book. Or conversely if you are taking flowers from this book and using them in a project from *Exploring Elizabethan Embroidery* then the flowers from this book, *Elizabethan Needlework Accessories*, will need to be scaled up in size.

With the inspiration of this book, give your imagination free rein, stitch and enjoy the pleasure of a technique originally enjoyed many centuries ago!

NECESSITIES

FABRICS

The embroidery in this book is worked on a variety of different fabrics including silks, satins, linen and velvet. This is very much as it was in the sixteenth and seventeenth centuries. To strengthen the fabrics they are always worked 'backed' and instructions are given for backing the fabrics. This ensures that the fabric used does not 'pull' with the weight of the embroidery worked on its surface.

THREADS

A variety of threads is used and the joy of this embroidery is that it can be worked in a thread weight that you feel comfortable with, from stranded cottons to rayon threads, hand-dyed and silk threads.

The range of threads now available is riches indeed! In the stitch guides we give the DMC rayon number (remove the first 3 or 30 and you have the correct stranded cotton number), the Anchor stranded cotton numbers and the Au Ver a Soie D'Alger and Perlee numbers. D'Alger thread will give a smooth sheen, Perlee is used to give textural interest to the raised work.

I have used rayon thread extensively as I like its sheen and I found the new DMC Rayon threads quite easy to use. One thread of rayon equals two threads of stranded cotton if you prefer to use stranded cotton.

There are so many beautiful threads available now - do not be limited to the threads listed in our stitch guides, use these as a guide and experiment with the many threads available. Random dyed threads have been used and these vary from shop to shop and country to country, so use whatever you have available near you.

Gold threads and cords are used extensively. This is entirely in keeping with embroidery in the Elizabethan period which was very rich with rubies and pearls sewn on as well as much gold thread. The gold cords and threads have all been couched in position and full instructions are given for this. In the stitch guides I have given three different weights of gold cord and thread that I particularly recommend. If you can't get the particular threads I recommend, buy whatever is available in your favourite needlework shop of the correct weight.

NEEDLES

A reasonably limited range of needles is used to work this embroidery. Crewel No.s 8, 9 and 10 are used with the rayon thread, fine metallic gold thread and the heavier threads. Tapestry No. 24 and 26 needles are used for the needlelace and may be used for the raised work embroidery. Beads may need to be sewn on with special beading needles though usually the crewel No. 10 needles will suffice. A large eyed darning needle may be useful when couching for taking the heavier gold cords to the back of the fabric.

BEADS

Precious and semi-precious stones were originally attached to Elizabethan work. Nowadays a similar effect can be achieved by using some of the beads that are available. These come in a very wide range of colours and sizes giving lots of scope to the modern embroiderer.

Scissors

You will need dressmakers scissors for cutting the fabric, a little pair of embroidery scissors for cutting threads and kitchen scissors for cutting out the templates.

Backing

Backing your main fabric is required to strengthen it. The backing also provides a most useful extra layer to start and finish threads into which will not show through to the front. To 'back' lay the main fabric on top of the backing very carefully, smooth out the wrinkles and then put into the frame together, stretching tightly. Do not stitch the backing and main fabric together as they often pull in different directions when put in the frame. When using velvet which would be damaged by a frame, stretch the backing material into the frame and then tack the velvet to the backing.

Embroidery Frames

The use of metallic threads, rich silk, satin or velvet and beads means that an embroidery frame is an absolute necessity. The work CANNOT be crushed into a hoop a section at a time. The whole design to be embroidered has to fit within the frame in its entirety. In Elizabethan times huge frames were used for this kind of work with the whole design drawn out ready to be worked and several people working on them at once.

If your frame is too large for your embroidery, take a larger piece of backing fabric which does fit your frame, stretch it tightly into your frame and then tack your main fabric piece onto the backing material in the frame.

There are many different types of commercial frames available and the choice of a frame is up to you but you *must use* a frame. I do not recommend slate frames as they seem to be a little large nor do I recommend plastic clip on frames as these go slack too quickly. I recommend a rectangular frame that takes the entire piece to be embroidered. Personally I staple my fabric very tightly onto a rectangular frame and leave it there until the work is completed. The work is beautifully taut to work on. Of course extra fabric has to be allowed for the staples to go through, this is trimmed off on completion of your embroidery.

If you use a hoop - and for small pieces they can be adequate - tighten the screw very firmly with a screw driver.

Transferring the design

There are many different ways of transferring designs to fabric, necessary because of the many different types of material used for embroidery - from fine silk to dark coloured linen and velvet.

Tracing the design

If your fabric is fine and light coloured you can literally trace the design from the book to the fabric. I use a fine lead pencil such as one of the 'clutch' or propelling drawing pencils that are cheaply available. These work well as they do not smudge or become messy, making your threads dirty, as do conventional pencils. Of course the pencil should be used carefully and lightly, *avoid making any more marks than are absolutely necessary.*

Trace only the main outlines of the design, do not transfer any fine details as these will not be hidden by subsequent stitching and these projects *are not washed* on completion

THE LIGHT BOX METHOD

Place the design to be traced on the glass, Position the design on your fabric with care, and trace the main outlines of the design only.

If you do not have a light box there are alternatives. Photocopy the design, darken with a black felt tip pen, tape it to your window and then tape the fabric over the top of the design and trace. Or use a glass table with a lamp underneath it to create light box conditions. By using a light box even the Brittney linen used in this book can be seen through.

SEWING CARBON PAPER

Trace the design from the book onto paper. Then place a piece of sewing carbon paper on top of your fabric, place the design on top of that. Trace the design onto your fabric with a fine tip, (preferably used up) ball point pen or something similar.

DOUBLE TRACING METHOD

Using a lead pencil, trace the design onto ordinary tracing paper, turn the tracing paper over and retrace the design on the back. Lay the tracing right side up onto the fabric and trace over the design again with your pencil. This leaves a faint copy on the fabric which can be drawn over again if required.

TEMPLATE SYSTEM

I use the template system, cutting out the shapes, then pinning and tacking round them for raised work and for velvet in particular. I find it the most satisfactory way of achieving good shapes on velvet.

To transfer a design by the template method, trace a template for each flower (including the stem and side leaves), cut out and position the flower where required. Note that the flower to be traced is simplified as additional details can be added when stitching. Cut the stem to shape on one side of the paper only, this way it is much easier to tack the stem outline.

When you are happy with the position of the flower, tack around the edge. You may find this is sufficient tacking to enable you to position the petals correctly. If you prefer you can trace a template of each petal in the flower and tack round that also. Keep the petals that are to be used for raised work to one side as these can be used as templates to cut the felt required. To ensure uniformity you can cut just one petal template and move it to each position. Remove the tacking threads once the main petals are stitched.

You may prefer to tack small sections at a time. For example the strawberry - cut out a template just of the strawberry fruit, cut it out in felt, attach to the background and embroider in raised work. (Take extra care with positioning the design when you do not transfer it all at once.) Next make a template of the small leaves behind the strawberry at the top. Pin into place, tack leaf outlines then embroider the leaves. Next make a template of the stem curve, cutting along the line of the curve and leaving the paper on one side, pin here. Tack the stem curve and then couch the gold cord in position. Continue in this way for the remaining embroidery.

Experiment and find which method suits you best.

ENLARGING AND DECREASING THE SIZE OF THE DESIGN

There are two very easy ways for changing the size of the designs given here and a third, not quite so easy.

• Make the distance between the border or edge and the embroidery design larger or smaller.

• Enlarge or reduce the design itself on the photocopier. The availability of photocopiers means that these tend to be used more nowadays. The traditional method of enlarging the design by drawing a grid pattern through it, then drawing a similar grid either larger if you want the design bigger, or smaller if you want the design smaller is an effective but time consuming method of adjusting the size of designs.

• Another method would be to adjust the distances between the flowers, leaves and curves. To do this trace off the individual flower (for instance) and move it further away (or closer) from the curves of the main outlines. Likewise with individual leaves etc to suit the new size needed. It is just a matter of re-spacing.

FINISHING OFF

Always embroider your name or at least your initials and the date of the completion of your embroidery in a corner of the completed article. It makes your embroidery that much more interesting and valuable in the years ahead.

HANDY HINT

Do not wash any of this embroidery.

If embroidery gets dusty - a light vacuum is the answer - cover the end of the hose with a fine clean cloth then hold over the embroidery and the dust will be lifted away without any damage to your embroidery.

HANDY HINT

When using DMC Gold or silver thread I dab the cut end, where the threads have a tendency to separate, onto my UHU glue stick. Take care as this work is not washed on its completion.

FISHBONE STITCH

ALSO CALLED LEAF SATIN

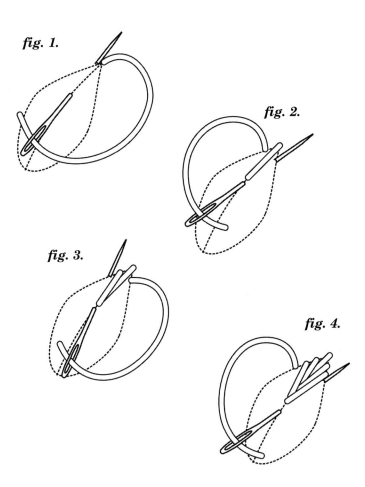

fig. 1.

fig. 2.

fig. 3.

fig. 4.

Fishbone stitch gives a nice smooth appearance to your stitching and serves as a foil to other heavier, more textured stitching. I find it a most useful stitch (especially for filling leaves) as it is easier to do neatly than satin stitch but gives the same effect. It is stitched using a crewel No. 9 or 10 needle.

To start bring the thread through at the tip of the leaf and make a straight stitch *approximately a third of the length of the shape to be filled* along the centre line of the shape (fig. 1).

Bring the thread through again to the left of the thread at the tip of the leaf and make a sloping stitch taking the needle down at the centre just below the point where the first stitch finished (fig. 2). Bring the thread through at the right of the first stitch and make a similar sloping stitch (fig. 3).

Continue working alternately on each side until the shape is filled (fig. 4). Stitches should be worked closely together.

SATIN STITCH

Satin stitch is a stitch that is used to great effect in many different styles of embroidery. Stitch using a crewel No. 9 or 10 needle.

This stitch should be worked with close even stitches to cover the fabric completely. Work the stitches on an angle across the area outlined and do not make the stitches too long or pull too tightly. It is easier to achieve a nice angle to your stitching if you start in the middle of the shape (fig. 1) and work to fill one side. Return to the centre and work in the opposite direction to fill the other side (fig.2).

Satin stitch can also be padded, this makes the work slightly raised which serves to emphasise the design. To work padded satin stitch the area must first be worked in running stitch to create the padding, satin stitch is then worked over the top (fig. 3). Care must be taken to keep the edge even.

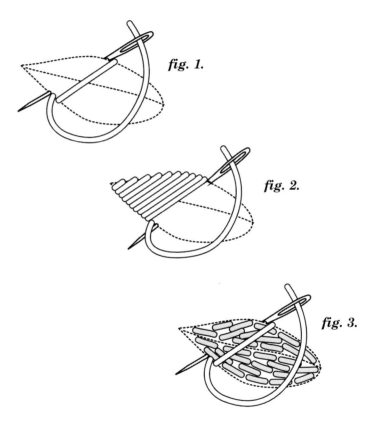

fig. 1.

fig. 2.

fig. 3.

LONG AND SHORT STITCH

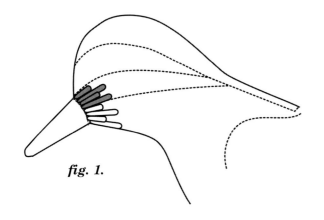

fig. 1.

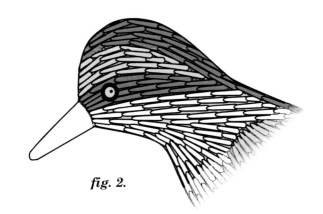

fig. 2.

This stitch is ideal for giving a solid block of colour. It can also be used most effectively for blending in colours and tone. It is a little like painting but instead of using paint and a brush you are using a needle and thread.

Stitch using a crewel No. 9 or 10 needle. In the first row the stitches are alternately long and short and closely follow the outline of the shape (fig. 1). The stitches in the following rows are all the same length but go *down through* the stitches in the preceding row. A regular outline is created by the foundation row while the inner rows produce an irregular line which allows colours to blend well without strongly defined lines.

The stitches follow the shape to give a natural flow to the design. Fill in closely so that there are no gaps showing through. When working long and short stitch on a very curved area you will find extra stitches are required to fill in gaps (fig. 2). This is very important when working the Kingfisher thimble but is necessary when working the petal shapes also.

PICOT AND EXTENDED PICOT STITCH

Picot stitch is a most useful and versatile surface stitch used in a variety of stitching techniques to create quite different three-dimensional effects, from perfect petals to long and twisted braid like shapes.

You may find it easier to stitch if you bring your thread through the fabric with a crewel No. 9 or 10 needle but change to a tapestry No. 24 needle for the weaving.

Work this stitch in a frame or hoop as a firm base is needed for both the stitched end and the pin. Anchor the thread at the back of your work then bring the thread to the front at A. Loop thread under pin before taking your thread down at B (fig. 1).

Bring thread back up in the middle between A and B at point C and take thread down and around pin (fig. 2).

Now weave the thread under B, over C under A (fig. 3). Reverse on the return row of weaving go over A, under C and over B (fig.4). Continue back and forth in this manner (fig. 5), pushing the weaving down all the time so that it is "tightly packed" when completed. Finish off by taking your thread through to the back of the material and work a couple of little back stitches to neaten off.

The size of the picot can be as long or as small as you like and to make *extended* picot stitch all that is required is that the pin is positioned further away from points 'A and 'B'.

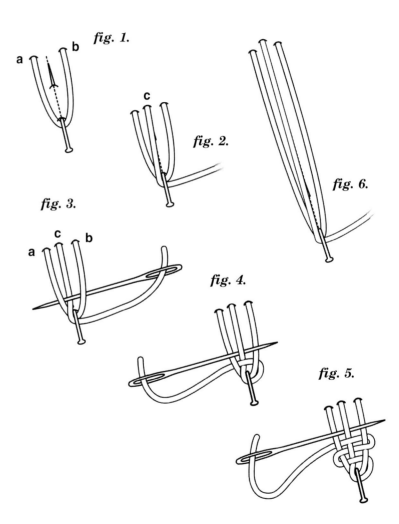

fig. 1.

fig. 2.

fig. 6.

fig. 3.

fig. 4.

fig. 5.

COUCHING

HANDY HINT

Pinch the laid thread between your fingers at leaf tips to make a sharp point.

In Elizabethan times metallic thread was used frequently and it is generally better couched in place than sewn. Sometimes all the embroidery is done first and the couched threads are applied last, other times you may feel you need to apply the couched threads first to give you the 'framework' of your design. The choice is up to you. Couching is quick to do, and most effective!

In couching two threads are used, the thread to be couched (laid) and the 'couching' thread which is stitched over the *laid thread* to hold the *laid thread* in the correct position and attach it to the fabric.

When couching it is common to use threads, cords and ribbons of a heavier weight, than those used elsewhere in the embroidery. (I have used three different weights of metallic cord and thread for couching in this book.) Sometimes it can be a challenge to bring the heavier cords through to the front of the embroidery ready to be couched in place and to take them through to the back when the stitching is complete. There are a *number of ways* to carry heavy threads through fabric.

• You can use a needle with a big eye (for example a large chenille needle).

• Or you may prefer to make a loop from a short length of strong thread (such as No. 3, 5 or 8 Perle). Thread the loop through the eye of a fairly large needle (chenille or a large darner) and then thread the end of the laid thread through the loop. Insert the needle through the fabric in the appropriate place and pull sharply. Like magic your thick thread goes through exactly where you want it!

• If the cord you are using is too heavy for either of the above methods, make a hole with an awl or stiletto then push the cord through the hole that has been made.

The heavier thread, cord or ribbon (which is the laid thread) needs to be secured in place at the back of the work at the beginning, and finished off when the embroidery is completed. It is best tacked down with ordinary sewing cotton and generally I use the couching thread to anchor the laid thread at the back of the work. I usually match the colour of the couching thread to the cord to be laid so that it will not be noticed.

As all of this embroidery is worked on backed fabrics, the laid thread can be secured at the beginning and end into the backing and these stitches will be completely invisible on the top of the work. If you have used a non iron-on interlining you can lift the backing away from the front material with your needle so the finishing off stitches don't show through on the front of the work. If you have used iron-on interlining just take care that your finishing off stitches do not come through to the front of the fabric.

It is easier to couch if your embroidery is held firmly in a frame. Plan to start couching at the base of the petal or leaf to be outlined. Place your laid thread where you wish to begin stitching then take the laid thread end to the back of your material using one of the methods outlined (fig. 1).

At the back of your work fasten the laid thread end securely into the backing using your couching thread (sewing cotton threaded in a sharp pointed needle) and stitch firmly.

Next bring the couching thread through to the front on the line to be couched 6 mm from the start and directly beneath the laid thread (fig 2). Remember to work from right to left. Take the couching thread over the laid thread and return back down through the fabric in the same position that you came up, actually *under* the laid thread (fig. 3). This makes the thread fit snugly round the laid thread and holds it firmly in place. All stitches are worked in a 'stab' fashion.

Continue couching the laid thread along the design line holding the laid thread in position with one hand and working couching stitches 6 mm apart (fig. 4). Remember to keep a little tension on the laid line.

When you are nearly at the end of the design line take your laid thread through to the back of your fabric before completing the last few couching stitches. Complete the last couching stitches then take the couching thread through to the back and sew down the end of the laid thread and finish off. I neaten my beginnings and endings as I go. This is not the traditional method but it does avoid any tangles under or on top of my work!

You will need to work the couching stitches more closely together when taking the laid thread around curves. When working round points always have a stitch at the tip and a stitch close to the tip on each side (fig. 5).

When your embroidery is completed it is backed with needlepunch to give a slightly raised, softer appearance to the embroidery. The needlepunch also ensures that the 'bulk' of the laid threads is not noticeable when the embroidery is completed as it is 'absorbed' into the needlepunch.

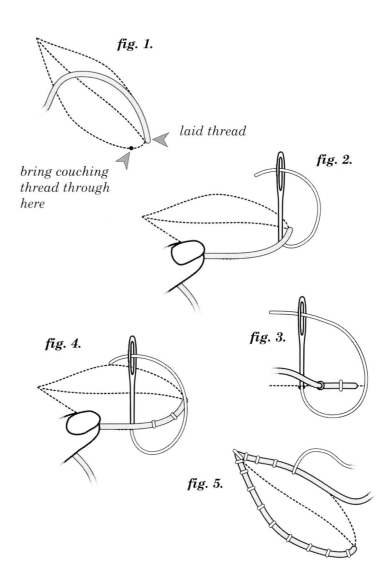

fig. 1.

laid thread

bring couching thread through here

fig. 2.

fig. 3.

fig. 4.

fig. 5.

SINGLE BRUSSELS STITCH

SINGLE BRUSSELS STITCH USED IN NEEDLELACE

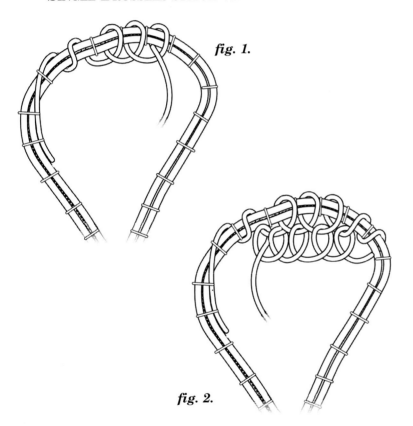

fig. 1.

fig. 2.

Single Brussels stitch is a much used stitch, it is also called detached buttonhole stitch and open buttonhole filling stitch. *Really it is just a simple detached buttonhole stitch.* It is used in many different stitch techniques and seems to have acquired a variety of names, so don't be put off by a different name it is really only a minor variation on buttonhole stitch.

In this book single Brussels stitch is used in needlelace and also in raised work embroidery. In both situations it is worked from left to right, then anchored, before the return row is worked from right to left. In needlelace it is anchored at the end of each row by wrapping the thread twice around the couched foundation thread. In raised work embroidery it is anchored by taking the needle through the fabric at the end of the row and bringing it back to the front one or two threads down from where it was taken through. Detailed information on using single Brussels Stitch in raised work embroidery is given on page 21.

To work single Brussels stitch to fill an area, for example the needlelace petals, start by running the thread up through the couching threads to the top of the petal.

Wrap the thread *around* the foundation thread on the left hand side as shown in fig. 1. Then buttonhole stitch across the foundation thread to the other side. Do not make the stitches too tight as the needle will need to go between these stitches easily when working the next row.

At the right hand side of the petal wrap the thread you are stitching with twice round the foundation thread. (One wrap to anchor and one wrap to cover.) Now work back across the row from right to left by working buttonhole stitches into the stitches in the row above (fig. 2).

Once back at the left hand side wrap the thread twice round the foundation thread as you did on the right hand side then buttonhole back across the petals. Repeat the last two rows back and forth until the section is filled. Increase and decrease as required.

To Increase

At times you will need to increase or decrease using this stitch to ensure your stitches cover the petal shape. To increase, work two buttonhole stitches into one loop. This can be done at the beginning and end of a row. You can also increase through the row if you need to (fig.3).

To Decrease

To reduce the width of your petal, or shape, you must reduce the number of stitches worked in each row. To do this work the first stitch into the second loop of the row above rather than the first, you may want to miss a loop or loops in the middle of the row also (fig. 4).

To Finish

To finish run the thread along through a few of the wraps that cover the foundation thread, as you did when starting.

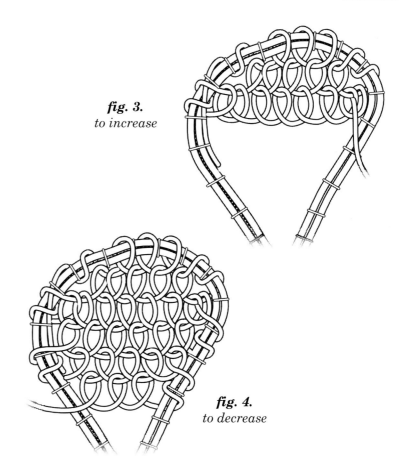

fig. 3.
to increase

fig. 4.
to decrease

NEEDLELACE ROSES

The Rose is a flower much loved by embroiderers and these three dimensional roses are particularly attractive. To make a needlelace rose using this technique the petals of the rose are created by working three separate layers of needlelace. The three layers are then stitched on to the fabric one layer on top of the other to create a rich, textured, many petalled rose. It is completed with a bead in the centre. The roses on the needle book and the book cover have been made in this way.

YOU WILL NEED

calico scraps - two pieces for backing - they only need to be a little larger than the design of the piece of needlelace to be made

- tracing paper and pencil
- clear contact
- sewing cotton for couching, to match embroidery thread
- sharp needle for sewing cotton used in couching and a tapestry needle for the needlelace
- embroidery thread

PREPARATION FOR NEEDLELACE STITCHING

Trace design on to paper and cover with contact. (This helps the needle slide over the surface.)

Place traced design on top of the two layers of calico then tack the two layers of calico and the tracing (covered with contact), all together. The two layers of calico give a firm surface to work on and make it easy to cut and unpick the couching stitches after you have made the needlelace.

AND NOW TO SEW!

Take thread the same colour as your subsequent needlelace filling will be, lay it round all the lines on the needlelace shape to be filled and double it, then add a little more thread for good measure. Now cut this length of thread off. (This doubled thread is your foundation thread and it is couched in place over all the lines on your traced outline.) It is important to *join up all the lines* with this thread as it holds the whole shape together. Detailed instructions are given with each piece of needlelace on the threads to use but for a trial I suggest using Coton a broder 16 for the foundation thread and also for the needlelace.

Thread a sharp sewing needle with sewing cotton that also matches your subsequent needlelace (double for strength) to be used for couching the foundation thread in place. This thread should match so that if you do not manage to pull all the little couching stitches out any stray threads won't show.

Anchor this couching thread (sewing cotton) very firmly at the back in the calico with a couple of back stitches. Now lay a doubled length of your foundation thread on the outline of the rose with the loop of the doubled thread adjacent to the centre, at the base of a petal (fig. 1). Bring the couching thread through to the front *and starting with a stitch through the centre of the looped end of the foundation thread,* continue couching the foundation thread around the petal leaving enough space for the needle to go between the couching stitches comfortably when the needlelace is being worked. Continue couching the foundation thread around the first petal until it joins the next petal (marked with an x).

At 'x' drop one thread and continue to couch down with a single thread until you reach the centre of the rose. Turn the thread back, making another loop, put a stitch here to secure then couch back to where you dropped the thread, couching on top of your previous stitching if possible (fig. 2). From this point pick up the dropped thread and continue couching over both strands until you reach the next petal. Continue, repeating the above procedure for each petal.

Non-separated petals

For a flower shape with non-separated petals begin couching as shown and continue round the whole shape with the double thread (fig. 3).

To finish the foundation thread

When the foundation thread is couched down all the way round the entire shape it must be securely fastened off. To do this divide the two foundation threads and couch one back along where you have just stitched for a little way, couching over the top of your earlier couching stitches. Cut that end of the foundation thread off. Couch back to where the remaining foundation thread is and to finish it off, couch it back in the direction you started from (fig. 4).

To finish the couching thread

To finish off your couching thread, take it to the back of your work and secure really firmly with a couple of back stitches into the calico.

It is important to remember that the foundation threads remain on the surface of your material at all times - this is the reason it begins with a loop and is finished by couching the two ends along the surface. The couching thread is the only thread allowed through the thicknesses of the paper design and calico. It is a tacking thread and will be cut and picked out when the needlelace is completed.

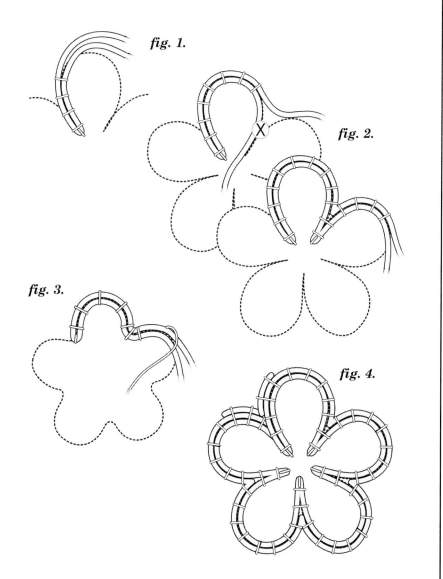

fig. 1.

fig. 2.

fig. 3.

fig. 4.

Needlelace filling using single Brussels stitch

Work Single Bussels stitch to create the needlelace filling. For more detailed information on how to embroider Single Brussels stitch see page 16. Work each petal separately always starting with a new length of thread.

The needlelace roses are made up of three separate layers of needlelace, in three different sizes. The biggest, bottom layer of rose petals is finished leaving a hole in the centre. This allows the other layers to 'sit' in the hole and helps to 'lift' the other layers into a slight 'cup' shape. The middle layer has a small hole left in the centre but the final and smallest layer is filled in completely with rounds of single Brussels stitch so that no hole is left at all. Fill to the centre of a layer of petals by working round the base of all the petals or leave a hole as required (fig. 6).

To finish

Finish the thread from each petal by running the thread along through a few of the wraps that cover the foundation thread in the same way as you did through the couching stitches when starting.

When all petals are completed, work buttonhole stitch round the outside edge of the petals. This gives a firm, neat edge and also secures any finishing off threads (fig. 6). The buttonhole edging can look most attractive worked in a metallic thread or a thread of a contrasting colour. A single strand of silk thread looks very delicate and flower thread also works well but it does lack a sheen. Choose the option that best suits your embroidery. For my roses I used a fine metallic thread. This stiffens the edge and helps the layers to stand up.

To assemble

Stitch the bottom layer on to your main fabric, with a few stitches of the same thread around the centre hole. Put the next layer on top, alternating the petals, stitch it down round the centre hole and pulling it into the hole a little. This will help to give the rose a nice shape. The top layer is attached in the centre, with a bead or decoration added to complete.

Changing thread in the middle of a petal

Start and finish at the beginning or end of a row. To finish off your thread run it through the couching. To start, run your thread up through the couching to where you will begin, subsequent stitching will secure this. Always aim to avoid more than one extra thread in the same place.

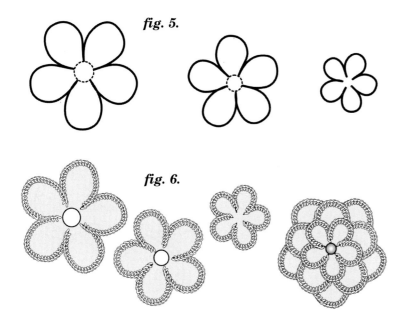

fig. 5.

fig. 6.

In Elizabethan Embroidery the stitchery is on the surface and to achieve the three dimensional effect which is so attractive, the stitchery is frequently padded. It can be padded as was shown in *Exploring Elizabethan Embroidery* by pushing a little dacron underneath the completed petal. Another way to achieve a raised, three dimensional effect is to pad the shape first and then stitch over the padding - raised work embroidery does this.

YOU WILL NEED

- tracing paper and pencil
- felt
- needle - Raised work embroidery is usually stitched using a crewel No. 8 or 9 needle, as this goes through the fabric easily, however if preferred a tapestry No. 24 needle can be used
- embroidery thread

There are five steps to creating raised work embroidery.

- Trace a template or pattern of the shape to be used, cut it out and use this pattern to cut a petal shape out of felt (fig. 1). Cut the shape *slightly smaller* than the design - certainly not larger.

- Tack felt shape in position with a couple of stitches (fig. 2). (Ideally use felt to match the thread to be used, though the felt will be covered with stitching so it doesn't really matter.)

- Use the same thread for the satin stitch that you will subsequently use for the needlelace. Start at the centre of the shape and satin stitch on the slant over the felt, stitch through the fabric *beside* the felt, not *through* the felt. This helps to give a *raised* look (fig. 3).

- Work single Brussels stitch over the satin stitch to cover the petal. Do not pull the stitches too tightly. When using single Brussels stitch in raised work embroidery the thread is anchored by taking the needle through the fabric at the end of each row, it

RAISED WORK EMBROIDERY

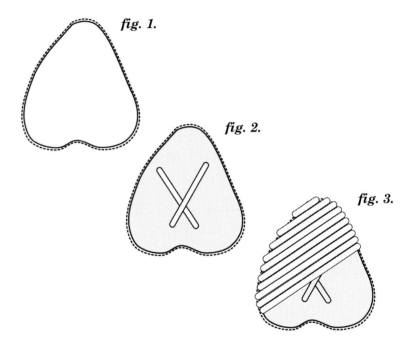

fig. 1.

fig. 2.

fig. 3.

HANDY HINT
Heavy duty vylene can be used instead of felt in fine work - it has the advantage that you can trace the outline straight on to it from the pattern.

SINGLE BRUSSELS STITCH AS USED IN RAISED WORK EMBROIDERY

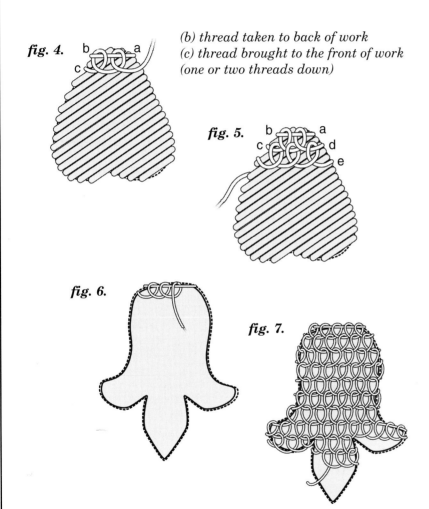

(b) thread taken to back of work
(c) thread brought to the front of work
(one or two threads down)

fig. 4.

fig. 5.

fig. 6.

fig. 7.

is then brought to the front one or two threads down from where it was taken through to the back, ready to continue stitching. Begin at the base of the petals by doing a straight stitch across the base point from (a) - (b) (fig. 4). Bring the thread back up to the front a few threads down at (c) and buttonhole over the thread 'bar' for as many stitches as it take to reach the end (usually about three). Take the thread down through the fabric at the end of the row at (d) (fig. 5) and come back up a couple of threads below where you went down at (e). Work single Brussels stitch back across the petal from right to left into the loops in the row above, then from left to right on the return row continue until the petal is completely covered. (For more detailed information on how to embroider single Brussels stitch see page 16.)

• If you prefer you can take the thread across the back of the fabric at the end of each row so that each row is worked in the same direction. Increase or decrease stitches as the design demands until the shape is covered. Refer to page 17 for detailed information on increasing and decreasing.

A CALYX OR SHAPED PETAL

When the petal or shape has a curved outer edge, start at the base of the shape (fig. 6). Work as far down the shape as you can, then work one side of the curve, or into the point of a calyx. When the first area is completed, take your thread through to the back of the work, then return your thread to the front of your work in the correct position to work the next curve or point. Continue in this way until all curves or points are completed (fig. 7).

TO START AND FINISH THREADS

It is easy to start and finish threads in raised work embroidery.

Start by doing a couple of little back stitches in the back of the work and then take your thread through to the front in the appropriate position. To finish, once again just take your thread through to the back of the work and work a couple of little back stitches.

Needle Book

A Needle Book is an absolute necessity for every embroiderer and this needle book is not only useful but also a most attractive piece of work to leave on display! Its inspiration came from a large sampler, of which this was only a very small part, worked in the mid seventeenth century. We have chosen the borage, pansy, carnation and rose for the front of our needle book but you could choose your favourite flowers from any of the flowers featured in this book or *Exploring Elizabethan Embroidery*.

You will need

- 40 cm square of green satin
- 2 small scraps of gold satin for the contrast
- 1 x 25 cm square of card or ice cream carton for stiffening
- fine poplin or lawn for backing to fit 18 cm frame
- bonding web e.g. Vlisofix
- 10 cm square of felt for padding flowers
- 20 cm square of needlepunch
- 20 cm square of heavy grade vylene
- 20 cm square of flannel for needle book pages
- 18 cm embroidery frame or 'hoop'
- 1.25 m of 3 mm wide gold metallic ribbon
- 10 cm of 1 cm wide gold metallic ribbon
- Beads - all gold: 7 seed, 3 flat beads or sequins, 5 tear drop and 1 larger bead to use as a catch to close the needle book, say 1 cm in diameter.
- Sewing cottons for tacking, lacing and construction
- Gutermann 968 or any good matching thread for couching on gold metallic threads
- Crewel Needles, No's 8, 9 and 10, Tapestry No. 24.
- General threads required listed with each flower
- fine gold metallic threads - such as Fil Light Gold DM 282 and Antique Gold DM 273
- DMC stranded gold thread for tassels

(finished size 12 x 14 cm)

Refer to the colour photograph on page 49 for additional detail.

Trace the design with a fine tipped pen or pencil to ensure that all markings are subsequently covered by your stitches

Actual size of needle book - trace outline for template

individual rose patterns to trace

Preparation

Cut a piece of green satin large enough to fit into an 18 cm embroidery hoop. Neaten the raw edges, then back with fine poplin or lawn fabric to strengthen. Refer to page 7 for detailed information on backing.

The front cover is to be worked on this fabric. Carefully trace a paper template of the 14 x 12 cm diamond shape. With contrasting cotton, tack round the template carefully, transferring the diamond shaped outline onto your fabric. Put the template to one side ready to be used when making up the needle book. Trace a pattern for the two contrasting diamonds then cut them out in the gold satin. Back with bonding web and remove the fabric from the hoop and iron the small diamonds into place. Replace the fabric *tightly* in the hoop.

Cut two 11 cm long pieces of 3 mm wide gold metallic ribbon and position over the raw edges of the gold satin to form the diamond areas where the flowers will subsequently be stitched. Fold the ends under and attach the ribbon to the cover. To do this sew with small stitches down the centre of the ribbon using a crewel No. 8 needle threaded with fine light gold metallic thread. Then stitch the 3 mm ribbon round the outside edges of the front cover in the same way.

Should you decide to substitute flowers from *Exploring Elizabethan Embroidery* you will need to reduce their size to the same size as the flowers given here.

To embroider the Flowers

I have used a combination of threads to embroider the flowers, including coton a broder 16 and rayon thread which has a nice sheen. Where rayon thread has been used I have used *one strand of rayon thread* only. *Two threads of stranded cotton* could be used instead of the rayon or the coton a broder 16. There are many other silk and hand dyed threads that could be most effective - use the threads that you enjoy working with, or branch out and try something new.

Transfer the flower shapes to the fabric using your preferred method. Refer to page 7 for detailed information on transferring designs.

The crewel No. 8 needle is used with the metallic and heavier thread, the crewel No. 9 with the rayon threads and the No. 10 with the sewing cotton. When doing raised work it is usually advisable to work with a crewel No. 8 needle as it goes through the fabric at the end of each row more easily, however a tapestry No. 24 needle can be used if preferred for raised work and needlelace.

Each of these flowers, except the rose has gold couching around and between each of the petals and sepals and around the calyx, where applicable. It has been stitched using fine light gold metallic thread, refer to the diagrams for additional details. Thread a crewel No. 8 needle with the metallic thread and a crewel No. 10 with the sewing cotton to be used for couching and you will find that you can do this quite quickly. For detailed information on couching refer to page 14.

Each Flower has full instsructions for its embroidery along with a shaded diagram to guide you when stitching.

Please Note

Throughout the text
* = DMC Rayon thread has been used. The numbers are the same as the stranded cottons except they have an additional '3' or '30' in front of the stranded cotton number.

BORAGE

Thread	DMC rayon	Anchor stranded cotton	Au Ver a Soie D'Alger	Perlee
leaf green	30472*	254	2142	
warm gold	30676*	891	2611	
brown	300	352	4216	302

Coton a broder 16
fine light gold metallic thread
antique gold metallic thread

Work the two large central petals first in fishbone stitch using warm gold. The vein is worked in straight stitches using antique gold metallic thread, refer to the diagram for details.

Cut felt templates of the three other large petals, these are stitched in 'raised work' using brown throughout. Work the gold petals on top in single Brussels stitch using fine light gold metallic thread.

The five small outer sepals have been worked in fishbone stitch using leaf green.

Using fine gold thread couch around the gold petals on top of the brown petals as well as round all the other petals. Complete with a flat gold bead and topped off with a seed bead.

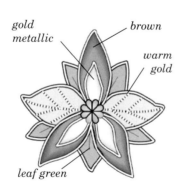

gold metallic — *brown*
warm gold
leaf green

PANSY

Thread	DMC rayon	Anchor stranded cotton	Au Ver a Soie D'Alger	Perlee
fawn	30738*	372	4222	
dark green	30895*	1044	1846	
light brown	301	1049	4215	525

Coton a broder 16
fine light gold metallic thread

Work the three large petals first in raised work using light brown.

The two lower petals have been worked in padded satin stitch, starting at the centre of each petal and using fawn. By starting your satin stitch at the centre of the petal it is easier to achieve the angle of stitching that you want.

The five sepals have been worked in fishbone stitch using dark green.

Couch with fine gold thread around the petals and sepals of the pansy and work the straight stitches radiating out from the centre of the three bigger petals with the same thread. Complete with a gold seed bead sewn on top of a large flat gold bead at the centre, refer to the diagram for detail.

light brown
dark green — *fawn*

CARNATION

Threads	DMC rayon	Anchor stranded cotton	Au ver a soie D'Alger	Perlee
fawn	30738*	372	4222	
warm gold	30676*	891	2611	
fine light gold metallic thread				

The two outer petals have been worked in long and short stitch using warm gold, with the inner petal stitched in the same manner using fawn. The first row of stitches closely follows the outline of each petal. Ignore the calyx when you stitch the petals as the calyx will be worked over the top of the base of these petals.

The calyx is worked in single Brussels stitch using fine light gold metallic thread and starting at the base. Work up to the three points stitching each one separately and bringing the points up over the top of the base of each petal. Detailed information on stitching a calyx is given on page 22.

Using fine gold thread couch around the petals and the calyx. Couch the curves at the base of the design also. Sew three gold seed beads on the tips of the calyx to complete.

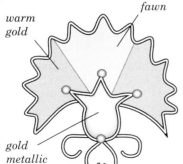

warm gold *fawn*

gold metallic

ROSE

Thread	DMC	Anchor stranded cotton	Au Ver a Soie D'Alger	Perlee
warm cream	677	386	2542	147
Coton a broder 16				
fine light gold metallic thread				

The rose is made up of three layers of needlelace worked in warm cream. Trace the outlines for the rose given on page 24 and refer to page 18 for full instructions on stitching a needlelace rose. Use the Coton a broder 16 for the foundation thread and matching sewing cotton for couching.

Upon completion of the needlelace petals buttonhole stitch around the edge of each of the petal layers in fine light gold metallic thread.

Then stitch the largest layer of petals to the centre of the green diamond, followed by the two other layers with the smallest at the top. Remember to alternate the placement of the petals.

Complete with one flat gold bead and one gold seed bead for the centre and 5 tear drop beads between back petals. Refer to the diagram for the placement of the tear drop beads.

all petals warm cream

To Make Up

Cut out the front cover, which features your embroidery, adding an extra 2 - 3 cm beyond the tacked line all round to lace over the stiffening. Cut three more pieces out of the green satin the same size as the front cover. These will form the inside and outside back cover and inside front cover.

Using the main template cut two diamonds from stiff card or plastic for the covers. Cut two similar diamonds from needlepunch, attach to stiff card or plastic (I use double sided Sellotape just to hold it in place as I lace). Place the needlepunch side of one cover to the back of the trimmed embroidered work and lace across the back keeping the corners neat. Repeat using *one* of the pieces of green satin cut out earlier, this will be the outside back cover. Check that the front and back match. Stitch the 3 mm edging ribbon round the back cover in the same way that you stitched the edging ribbon for the front cover.

Cut 2 diamonds of heavy vylene 5 mm smaller (finished size 13.5 x 11.5 cm) and lace the two remaining pieces of satin over each one. These are then stitched to the inside of the front and back covers as invisibly as possible. (Avoid slanting stitches for a neat finish.)

When stitching the front cover together insert a 6 - 8 cm loop of 3 mm ribbon between the lining and the cover at the right hand point to act as a loop to go over the bead to be sewn on the back cover. This will hold the needle book closed.

Hinge

The hinge is made from a 10 cm length of 1 cm wide gold ribbon. Fold under the ends and using Gutermann 968 (or any sewing thread that is a good colour match to the ribbon) slip stitch one edge of the ribbon to the front cover edge along the top left hand side of the diamond (just beside the 3 mm ribbon already sewn on) and then slip stitch the other edge to the corresponding edge of the back cover.

Inside pages

Cut as many pages as required a little smaller than the template. Neaten with nun's stitch or four sided stitch and stitch onto the inside back cover along the top left-hand side. You may find that your 'book' closes more neatly if you 'stagger' the attachment of the pages. To do this attach one at the very edge of the cover, attach the next about 6-8 mm from the edge and so on. If you do this you will have to adjust the size of the pages.

Tassels

The finishing touch on the needle book is the addition of the three little tassels made with DMC stranded gold metallic thread. Stitch the tassels to the left, right and bottom front points and your needle book is complete!

Handy Hint

Sandpaper the sharp points at the corners of the diamond stiffening as if left sharp the points will protrude through the fabric.

PIN CUSHION

A Pin Cushion is an absolute necessity in every needleworker's set of accessories. This pin cushion has been embroidered on velvet, a material that was very popular as a base for embroidery in the seventeenth century but not used so much now. The lush appearance that velvet gives to your embroidery makes it worth the extra effort involved in transferring the design. We give very clear instructions for transferring the design. Follow these and I am sure you will find making this pin cushion a most enjoyable experience. Of course the designs could also be used as motifs on a bell pull, or individually on a brooch - the scope is unlimited!

YOU WILL NEED

- 20 cm x 1 m of material, we have used velvet but silk or satin also work well
- 1 m fine backing - lawn or poplin
- 10 cm square heavy vylene
- Wool fleece to stuff the pin cushion
- Seven hexagonal templates as for patchwork, plastic ice cream containers are ideal
- 15 cm or larger embroidery frame (must be larger than the design to be embroidered)
- Crewel No.s 8, 9, and 10, Tapestry No. 24
- Gutermann 968 or any good matching thread for couching on gold metallic threads
- Sewing thread to match the main fabric
- A complete list of embroidery threads used is given in the Thread Guide
- Three different thicknesses of gold metallic cord and thread:
  - 1 m x 2 mm *craft gold metallic* - referred to as 'heavy' cord
  - 1 m x 1 mm *crinkle gold metallic cord* - referred to as 'medium' cord
  - *Fil light gold thread DM 282* - referred to as fine gold metallic thread
- Beads - 5 gold leaf beads, 2 flat gold beads, 3 x 2 mm gold beads, gold and mauve seed beads

(finished size 9 x 12 cm)

Refer to the colour photograph on page 50 for additional detail

PLEASE TRACE THESE FLOWERS

Blue Borage

Pansy

Thistle

Strawberry

Bronze Borage

Carnation

PREPARATION

Trace the hexagon pattern with the solid outline given (fig. 1). With this as your template cut seven hexagons from plastic or card and one from the heavy vylene exactly the same size as the template. Your embroidery will be stretched over the plastic or card when completed. The top of the pin cushion is laced over the vylene.

Now cut eight pieces of material using the template above but adding a 1.5 cm seam allowance all round - this will be turned under when the embroidery is completed.

Velvet fabric has a pile that would be damaged if it was stretched and held firmly in a frame. To avoid damaging the material stretch your backing fabric firmly into the frame and then tack the velvet onto the backing fabric. For detailed information on backing please refer to page 7.

TO TRANSFER THE DESIGNS

Tack the outline of the hexagon on to the velvet. This acts as a frame for each flower and helps you to place each flower correctly. *Remember to place the flower so that the template has a flat side, top and bottom (fig. 2).* The outline tacking is not removed until the material has been laced over the template.

The designs to be traced are given on page 30.

Different ways of transferring designs are given on page 7. We recommend the template method for transferring designs to velvet. It can be used reliably and easily and you will find you no longer avoid using velvet.

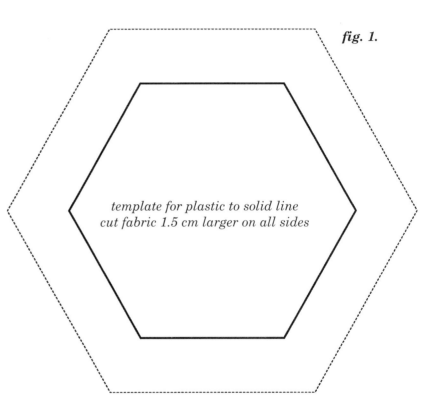

fig. 1.

*template for plastic to solid line
cut fabric 1.5 cm larger on all sides*

HANDY HINT

The clear plastic lids of ice cream containers are ideal as templates as when the embroidery is being worked in the hoop, you can hold the 'clear' template over the top to check the placing and size of your embroidery.

HANDY HINT

Remember there has to be a flat side at the top and bottom of the hexagon when positioning your flower.

fig. 2.

PLEASE NOTE

* DMC Rayon thread has been used. The numbers are the same as the stranded cottons except they have an additional '3' or '30' in front of the stranded cotton number.

TO EMBROIDER THE FLOWERS

I have used mainly rayon thread to embroider the flowers as the sheen of the rayon enhances the richness of the velvet. There are many other silk and hand dyed threads that could be used most effectively.

The crewel No. 8 needle is used with the metallic and heavier thread, the crewel No. 9 with the stranded cottons and rayon and the No. 10 with the sewing cotton. When doing raised work it is usually advisable to work with a crewel No. 8 needle as it goes through the fabric at the end of each row more easily, however a tapestry No. 24 needle can be used if preferred and is best for needlelace.

Medium gold cord has been couched on to each flower to create stems and tendrils. Fine gold thread has been couched round the outside of each flower, leaf etc. This is stitched as each flower is completed. Refer to page 14 for detailed information on couching.

One strand of rayon thread has been used for all raised embroidery. Two strands have been used for fishbone stitch and padded satin stitch. Two strands of thread are used on velvet (whereas one strand would be used on silk or satin) as the threads can be 'lost' in the velvet pile. One strand of rayon thread equals two threads of stranded cotton.

Each flower has full instructions for its embroidery along with a shaded diagram to guide you when stitching.

BLUE BORAGE

Thread	DMC rayon	Anchor stranded cotton	Au Ver a Soie D'Alger	Perlee
white	30762*	1	optic white	blanc
mid blue	30322*	142	4923	417
light blue	33325*	140	4922	

Work the two upper side petals first in fishbone stitch using mid blue.

Cut felt templates of the three large petals. These are stitched in 'raised work' using light blue throughout. Work the petals on top in single Brussels stitch using white thread.

The five small outer sepals have been worked in fishbone stitch using light blue.

Using medium gold cord couch the main stem of the borage. Use fine gold metallic thread to couch round all the petals but not the sepals. With the same thread work the veins on the two petals worked in fishbone stitch in straight stitches and the straight stitches coming out from the sepals. Refer to the diagram for details. A small gold bead has been sewn at the centre of the borage to complete it.

mid blue *light blue* *white*

PANSY

Thread	DMC rayon	Anchor stranded cotton	Au Ver a Soie D'Alger	Perlee
fuchsia pink	33608*	85	3032	345
dark fuchsia pink	33607*	87	3045	
light sea green	30504*	875	1822	

Work the three large petals first in raised work using fuchsia pink.

The two upper petals have been worked in padded satin stitch, starting at the centre of each petal and using dark fuchsia pink. (Remember to use two threads). By starting your satin stitch at the centre of the petal it is easier to achieve the desired angle of stitching.

The four sepals and lower leaf have been worked in fishbone stitch using light sea green

Using medium gold cord couch the stem. Outline the petals, leaf and sepals using fine gold metallic thread and sew a small gold bead on top of a flat gold bead to mark the flower centre.

dark fuchsia pink *light sea green* *fuchsia pink*

Thistle

Thread	DMC rayon	Anchor stranded cotton	Au Ver a Soie D'Alger	Perlee
olive green	30469*	268	2136	378
thistle head - a variegated mauve to purple thread is ideal				
but a selection of	33607*	87	3045	132
threads can be used	30211*	342	3311	348
	553	110	3314	434
light green	30368*	208	5023	
fine gold metallic thread				

Work the base first in raised work using olive green.

The thistle head is worked in straight stitches using either a variegated mauve to purple thread or threads selected randomly from those listed above. When you have created a nice dense thistle head embroider French knots, using the same threads, across the top.

The lower leaf has been worked in fishbone stitch using light green.

Using medium gold cord couch the stem, leaf stem and 'curls' at the edge of the thistle. The design on the base of the thistle has been made with fine metallic thread laid diagonally in long straight stitches across the area. Where the stitches cross they have been held down with a small straight stitch also worked in fine gold thread.

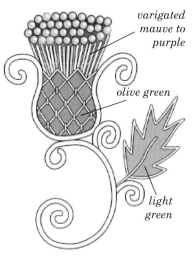

varigated mauve to purple

olive green

light green

Strawberry

Thread	DMC rayon	Anchor stranded cotton	Au Ver a Soie D'Alger	Perlee
bright red	30349*	46	935	681
light green	30368*	208	5023	
side leaf a variegated green blue pink thread was used - substitute light green				

The strawberry has been stitched in raised work using bright red.

The sepals and side leaf have been worked in fishbone stitch. The sepals using light green and the side leaf using a variegated thread. Light green is an effective substitute for the varigated thread.

Using medium gold cord couch the stem. Couch round the edge of the strawberry. The sepals and the side leaf using fine gold metallic thread. The strawberry is completed by the addition of gold seed beads where indicated. Refer to the diagram for their placement.

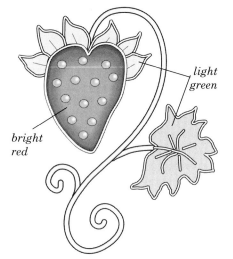

light green

bright red

BRONZE BORAGE

Thread	DMC	Anchor stranded cotton	Au Ver a Soie D'Alger	Perlee
rust	919	340	2626	203
tan	921	338	2624	
soft pink	30754*	868	2641	
Kreinik Balger antique copper Braided Cord No. 16				

The centre top petal has been worked in raised work using rust.

The two top side petals (one each side) have been worked in satin stitch using tan and the three front petals have been worked in fishbone stitch using soft pink.

Antique copper cord has been couched round the raised work petal and down into the centre of each of the other petals. Refer to the diagram for additional detail.

The main stem has been couched in medium gold cord with fine gold metallic thread couched round all the petals except the top one. To complete, sew eight gold seed beads where indicated, at the base of the top petal.

tan *rust* *soft pink*

CARNATION

Thread	DMC rayon	Anchor stranded cotton	Au Ver a Soie D'Alger	Perlee
fresh pink	30899*	41	2944	307
maroon	30814*	44	2926	
light green	30368*	208	5023	
fine gold metallic thread				

The three large petals have been worked in single Brussels stitch using fresh pink and taking care to stitch into the points. (Instructions for doing single Brussels stitch are given on page 16 and for help on stitching into points refer to page 22). When you stitch the petals ignore the calyx as it will be worked over the top of the petals.

The four long narrow petals have been worked in straight stitches using maroon. The leaves are worked in fishbone stitch using light green.

The calyx is worked in single Brussels stitch using fine light gold metallic thread and starting at the base. Work up to the points stitching each one separately and bringing the points up over the top of the base of each petal. Detailed information on stitching a calyx is given on page 22.

Couch the main stem using medium gold cord and couch round all the petals and leaves using fine gold metallic thread.

fresh pink *maroon* *gold metallic thread* *light green*

NEEDLELACE ROSE

Thread	DMC rayon	Anchor stranded cotton	Au Ver a Soie D'Alger	Perlee
light raspberry pink fine gold metallic thread	33689*	74	3021	494

The rose is made up of three layers of needlelace worked in light raspberry pink. Trace the given outlines for the rose and refer to page 18 for full instructions on stitching a needlelace rose. Use a doubled length of the rayon thread for the foundation thread and matching sewing cotton for couching. The single Brussels stitch is worked using one thread.

Upon completion of the needlelace petals buttonhole stitch around the edge of each of the petal layers in fine gold metallic thread.

Then stitch the largest layer of petals to the centre of the hexagon, followed by the two other layers with the smallest at the top. Remember to alternate the placement of the petals.

A gold leaf has been placed where indicated beneath the petals and the centre of the rose has been completed with a flat gold bead topped with a gold seed bead. Refer to the diagram for further details.

diagrams to trace

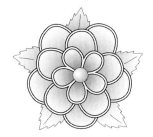

all petals light raspberry pink

HANDY HINT

When using metallic threads, (the kind we use in this book) especially when going round curves etc little 'kinks' can occur. To keep a nice flowing line, the laid thread sometimes needs a little 'tug' to keep it true to the line of your design.

TO MAKE UP

You should now have seven embroidered hexagons and an eighth hexagon cut out in velvet that is plain - embroider your initials and the date of completion on this plain hexagon which will be the base of your pin cushion.

Check that all the plastic or card hexagons are *exactly* the same size!

Trim each of the embroidered pieces and cut away surplus *backing* fabric to prevent too much bulk. Then lace each embroidered hexagon over the card or plastic. The lacing must be stretched over the hexagon *very tightly* as when the pieces are stitched together the hexagons 'spring' into the curves with the tension. The surplus material must be trimmed back, especially at the corners which can get too bulky and give your pin cushion a lopsided look. Stitch the corners securely, keeping them flat, after the lacing is done.

If the lacing is not very tight the fabric tends to pucker when it is concaved. The tight lacing makes stitching the pieces together very hard on your fingers and it also makes it difficult getting the needle through when couching but it is worth it.

Ladder stitch the six embroidered sides together in a circle. Stitch the top half of each side first (fig. 3), then stitch the bottom side second. Now each hexagon is concaved in shape. Couch heavy gold thread over each of the joins, the ends can be neatened at the back of your work and will be inside the pin cushion when completed. Couch with a 'stabbing' action rather than passing your needle in and out, in one action.

Next stitch the base onto the circle. Pin the base with a single pin in the centre of each side of the base hexagon to the corresponding side hexagon (fig. 4). Check that all sides are fitting together evenly. Slip stitch the base to the sides.

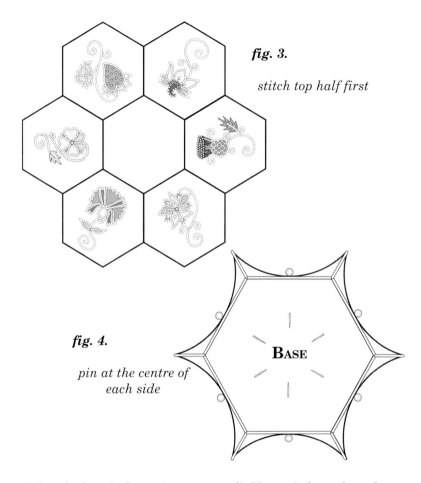

fig. 3.

stitch top half first

fig. 4.

pin at the centre of each side

BASE

Fill with sheep's fleece (unspun wool). Now stitch on the vylene covered top. It is easier to stitch the soft top on last. Couch heavy gold cord around the top poking the ends in at one corner. Your pin cushion is now complete.

SCISSOR OR SPECTACLES CASE

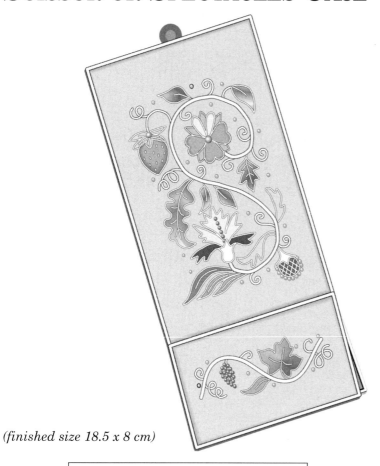

(finished size 18.5 x 8 cm)

Refer to the colour photographs on
pages 52-53 for additional detail

Scissors are an embroiderers' tool of the trade and really need
to go everywhere that an embroiderer goes!

This Scissors Case is beautifully embroidered on both sides so
that it is not only a most useful accompaniment for the
embroiderer, it is also a delight to behold. At the end of the
scissors case there are two little flannel pages to put your needles
in making this a most convenient little carry all for your sewing
requirements. It could also be made up as a spectacles case, with a
little cloth for cleaning your glasses at the end, instead of the
flannel.

YOU WILL NEED

- If you are going to make this up as a glasses case check the
  size of your glasses and adjust the length or width if required
- 25 cm square of main fabric (I used Brittney)
- 25 cm square of lining - this could be the same as the main
  fabric if desired
- lawn or poplin for backing fabric - cut big enough to fit your
  frame
- 1 small piece of flannel 8 x 7 cm for needle case pages or
  similarly sized appropriate cloth if to be used for a spectacle
  case
- Three different thicknesses of gold metallic cord and thread:
  - 2 m x 2 mm *craft gold metallic* - referred to as 'heavy' cord
  - 1 m x 1 mm *crinkle gold metallic cord* - referred to as
  'medium' cord
  - *Fil light gold thread DM 282* - referred to as fine gold
  metallic thread

PATTERN TO BE TRACED

ROSE

STRAWBERRY

2 cms *
not
stitched

12.5 cms
stitch back and front together from * - *

5 cms
for needlebook

8.5 cms

Top - left open

8.5 cms

together and form needlebook →

← machine here to join two sides

19.5 cms overall

- Gutermann 968 or any good matching thread for couching on gold cord
- Sewing thread the same colour as your main fabric for construction
- 25 cm embroidery frame, must be large enough to enclose entire design
- A complete list of the embroidery threads used is given in the Thread Guide - these are given as a guide only, feel free to substitute for your own favourite or preferred threads
- Beads Mill Hill seed and 1 mm Midnight Rainbow 00374, seed Antique Cranberry 03003, gold seed beads, 5 x 2 mm gold beads and 2 x 1 cm gold beads to serve as a catch.

TO TRANSFER THE DESIGN

The type of material that you are using for making this Scissor Case will influence your method of transferring the design. We give different ways of transferring the design on page 00. I traced using a light box and then even this 'Brittney' can be seen through.

PREPARATION

The main fabric on which the embroidery is stitched is not cut to size until the embroidery is completed.

Cut two pieces of backing fabric and two pieces of the main fabric big enough to fit the embroidery frame you are going to be working in (25 cm). Neaten the raw edges to prevent fraying and then 'back' to strengthen your fabric. Further information on 'backing' is given on page 7. One side of the scissors case will be worked on this fabric. (Put the other two pieces of fabric to one side until you are ready to work the second side of the scissors case.) Once the main fabric and backing fabric are on the frame, measure, then tack the outline for the finished size of the scissors case, including the needle case, onto the fabric (8.5 x 19 cm). The tacking will enclose your traced design.

TO EMBROIDER THE DESIGN

This Scissors Case is embroidered on both sides. One side is identified as the 'Rose' side and the second is the 'Strawberry' side. Separate instructions are given for working each side. Random dyed thread is used here to create interesting shading on the leaves. I have used *one strand of rayon thread* or Bravo thread. *Two threads of stranded cotton* could be used instead of the rayon, plus there are many other silk and hand dyed threads that could be used most effectively - use the threads that you enjoy working with, or branch out and try something new.

All satin, fishbone stitch and couching to be worked using a crewel No. 9 or 10 needle. You may also find this the easiest needle to use when working single Brussels stitch as it goes through the material at the end of each row more smoothly. Alternatively you could use a tapestry needle No. 24 which is also used for working the needlelace.

PLEASE NOTE
* DMC Rayon thread has been used. The numbers are the same as the stranded cottons except they have an additional '3' or '30' in front of the stranded cotton number.

SCISSORS CASE - ROSE SIDE

Thread	DMC	Anchor stranded cotton	Au Ver a Soie D'Alger	Perlee
cranberry	33350*	78	3025	
light raspberry pink	33689*	74	3021	
bright blue	30820*	134	116	
mid blue	30322*	131	4912	
leaf green	30472*	254	2142	
olive green	30469*	1268	2136	
maroon	30814*	44	2926	
salmon pink	30352*	10	2643	
dark red stranded cotton	815	43	2925	
medium Paris Pink	224	894	4622	177
Coton a broder 16				
Bravo A122				
variegated blue/tan	103/105	1211/ 1218	1736/4511 4521/4213	

LEAVES

All the leaves have been worked in fishbone stitch, refer to the diagram for the colours used.

LEAF KEY

▨	*leaf green*	🔲	*variegated turquoise / tan thread*
▩	*olive green*	🔲	*bright blue*

THE ROSE

First the background sepals are worked in fishbone stitch using cranberry. Take care that the petals are positioned correctly to be seen when the needlelace rose is attached - they should just 'peek' out from behind the petals.

The petals of the rose are made of needlelace worked in medium Paris pink. Trace the outline of the rose onto tracing paper and work following the instructions given on page 18. Use the thread used for the needlelace filling, doubled as the foundation thread and matching sewing cotton for couching. Outline the completed rose in buttonhole stitch using fine gold metallic thread and a crewel No. 8 needle. Attach to the main fabric where indicated on the design.

THREE SMALL PETALS ADJACENT TO IVY

These have been worked in padded satin stitch using one thread of dark red stranded cotton and starting at the centre of each petal for a better finish.

HONEYSUCKLE

The petals on this flower are all worked in padded satin stitch, starting at the centre of each petal and using maroon for five of the petals and light raspberry pink for four of the petals. Refer to the diagram for the variations in colours used on the petals.

rose pattern to trace

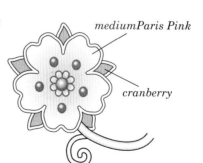

medium Paris Pink

cranberry

dark red

The tips of the four light raspberry pink petals have been stitched in single Brussels stitch using fine gold metallic thread.

Large Bud

The centre of this bud has been worked in padded satin stitch starting in the centre of the shape and using mid blue.

The calyx has been worked in single Brussels stitch using fine

metallic gold thread and starting by the stem. For more detailed information on stitching a calyx refer to page 22. While you have the fine gold thread in your needle, couch round the outer edge of the bud - the beads are best applied later.

Couching - Both sides

For detailed information on couching refer to page 14.

Heavy (2 mm) gold metallic cord has been used to couch on the main 'S' shape design. The scrolls and tendrils have been couched with medium (1 mm) gold cord.

Fine metallic gold thread has been couched around all the leaves and petals throughout. It has also been couched down the centre of leaves, refer to the diagram for details. This must be done at the completion of your embroidery, but before you apply the beads.

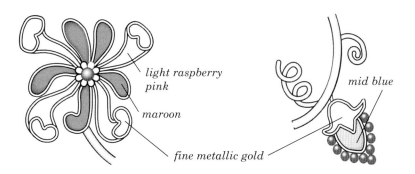

light raspberry pink

maroon

fine metallic gold

mid blue

Beads - Both sides

Beads, these are sewn on last - after the couching and all other stitching is completed, as otherwise your thread is constantly catching on them which is most annoying!

Gold seed beads have been sewn all over the background fabric, where indicated.

Rose side

Five Antique Cranberry beads, have been sewn on the rose where indicated with a larger, 2 mm gold bead sewn in the centre.

The grapes have been created using Midnight Rainbow beads, these have been sewn where indicated to create a lush bunch of grapes.

The three small petals adjacent to the ivy leaves and the honeysuckle both have a 2 mm gold bead sewn at their centre, refer to the diagram.

12 Antique Cranberry seed beads have been sewn around the outside edge of the large bud.

The grapes on the needle case section of the Scissors case have been created on the rose side using Midnight Rainbow seed beads and on the strawberry side Antique Cranberry seed beads have been used.

Strawberry side

The strawberry and pansy have a 2 mm gold bead sewn where indicated.

The carnation at the base of the embroidery has six Antique Cranberry seed beads, sewn up the centre of the flower, where indicated.

Around the edge of the pomegranate 12 gold seed beads have been sewn as a finishing touch.

SCISSORS CASE - STRAWBERRY SIDE

Thread	DMC	Anchor stranded cotton	Au Ver a Soie D'Alger	Perlee
maroon	30814*	44	2926	
cranberry	33350*	78	3025	
salmon pink	30352*	10	2643	
mid blue	30322*	131	4912	
bright blue	30820*	134	116	
light raspberry pink	33689*	74	3021	
olive green	30469*	268	2136	
leaf green	30472*	254	2142	
dark red	815	43	2925	109
Coton a broder 16				
Bravo A122				
variegated blue/tan	103/105	1211/ 1218	1736/4213 4511/4521	

LEAVES

All the leaves have been worked in fishbone sitich, refer to the diagram for the colours used.

LEAF KEY

▨ leaf green

▨ olive green

▨ salmon

▨ variegated turquoise/tan thread

▨ bright blue

THE STRAWBERRY

The Strawberry has been stitched in raised work in dark red. Full instructions for raised work are given on page 21.

The sepals have been worked in fishbone stitch using leaf green.

THE PANSY

The petals have all been worked in padded satin stitch using two different colours, starting at the centre of each petal. Work the lower three, heart shaped petals first in cranberry then the two top petals in salmon pink.

The five sepals in between the petals have been worked in fishbone stitch in mid blue.

CARNATION

This flower has been worked in long and short stitch, with the lower two petals worked first in maroon and the main section of the flower worked in light raspberry pink. The first row of stitches worked closely follows the outline of each petal.

Starting at the base, the calyx has been worked in single Brussels stitch using a fine gold metallic thread. (For more detailed information on stitching a calyx refer to page 22.)

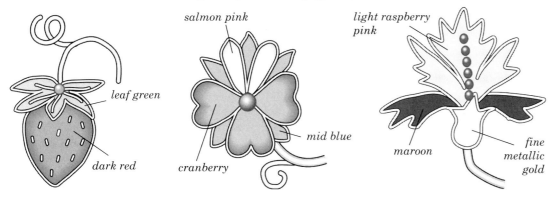

POMEGRANATE OR 'FANTASY' FLOWER

The central area has been completely covered with satin stitch worked using maroon thread. Start stitching in the centre of the flower and work out to each side. Fine gold metallic thread is then worked over the satin stitch in a trellis pattern. Work straight stitches with a small stitch at the intersection of the straight stitches to create the pattern, (refer to the diagram for details). Couch round the edge of the central area but do not apply the beads until your embroidery is completed.

fine metallic gold

maroon

Starting at the base, the calyx has been filled with single Brussels stitch worked in fine gold metallic thread. (For more detailed information on stitching a calyx refer to page 22.)

TO MAKE UP

The back and front of the scissors case are made up separately. They are both constructed in the same way and then joined together to create the scissor case.

With the embroidery completed, cut the main fabric with the embroidery on it, to the correct size of 10.5 x 21.5 cm. This includes an allowance of 1 cm all round for seams.

- Cut two pieces of lining the same size.

- With right sides facing (lining and embroidered fabric) machine stitch together three sides. Neaten the edges and trim the corners. Turn right side out.

- Press round the outside - *not* the embroidery!

- Turn in the top edge then slip stitch together.

- When both sides have been stitched in this way, join them together by machining across the width of the scissors case 5 cms up from the bottom, as indicated on the pattern. This forms the needle case.

- Leave 2 cm down from the top open then slip stitch the two long sides together using matching sewing cotton. (*Stop at the top of the needlecase!*)

- Couch the heavy (2 mm) gold metallic cord over the seams all the way round the entire scissor case and across the machine stitching which forms the needle case. Begin and end the couching by tucking away the ends of the metallic cord at the join of the needle case pages and at the opening at the top. (I couched these down a good 2.5 cm into the scissor case so that there was no risk of the heavy gold cord coming loose.)

- Neaten the flannel, by hand or machine, fold it in half before attaching with back stitches to the centre of the needle case.

- Sew the two 1 cm beads to the centre of the opening at the top, one on either side of the scissor case. Now make a little loop of the heavy gold metallic cord to fit over both beads, attach to one side of the scissor case around the bead on that side but leave it loose to catch over the bead on the other side. This will help to keep your scissors secure in their case. Your scissors case is now complete!

BOOK COVER

In Elizabethan times books were very precious and rare items that were looked after with great care. Richly embroidered covers were made to enhance books, usually the Bible, and an equally beautiful and richly embroidered bag would be made in which to keep the book to provide greater protection. When the book was in use it would often be rested on an embroidered cushion to protect it further! The embroidery varied from tent stitch to gold work to fine silk embroidery depending on the materials used for the book cover.

This book cover was inspired by covers of the past but uses up-to-date materials and freely available threads. It was designed to fit an A5 size diary or notebook. It is made to slip on and off so that it can be used from year to year. Being ornate, it is not intended to be stored on the book shelf with other books, but rather to lay decoratively on the table by your chair for use - and admiration!

YOU WILL NEED

- Approximately 80 x 30 cm of fabric - gold lame, silk, satin, velvet or fabric of your choice.
- 0.5 m of backing - lawn or poplin, large enough to fit frame
- Embroidery frame (must be larger than the design to be embroidered)
- Crewel No.s 8,9, and 10, Tapestry No. 24
- Gutermann 968 or any good matching thread for couching on gold metallic threads
- Sewing thread to match the main fabric
- A complete list of embroidery threads used is given in the Thread Guide.

(finished size 14.5 x 21 cm)

Refer to the colour photograph on page 51 for additional detail

- Three different thicknesses of gold metallic cord and thread:
  - 2 m x 2 mm *craft gold metallic* - referred to as 'heavy' cord
  - 1 m x 1 mm *crinkle gold metallic cord* - referred to as 'medium' cord
  - *Fil light gold thread DM 282* - referred to as fine gold metallic thread
- plus red metallic 1 ply 003 red Au ver a Soie a good substitute for this would be Kreinik red filament
- Beads - a variety of mixed coloured glass seed beads, 1 x 5 mm gold bead and 1 x 4 mm gold bead

This book cover is made in two parts. The embroidered front cover is made separately from the main book cover which is just plain material. The plain cover was made and slipped onto the book. Then the embroidered front cover was slip stitched onto the plain cover. This made it easier to position the embroidered front cover exactly where required. (It also meant a large frame was not needed, and the material not in use was safely out of harm's way!) Heavy (2 mm) gold cord was couched over the seam to complete.

Preparation and Transferring the Design

Cut a piece of material 25 x 20 cm from the fabric you have chosen for your book cover plus a piece of backing fabric the same size, or bigger if required, to fit the frame you plan to use. The finished size is 21 x 14.5 cm but the larger measurement given allows for a seam allowance plus extra to fit the size of the frame. I used a home made rectangular frame but use the type of frame you prefer that will take the complete design. For further information on framing your fabric please refer to page 7.

The type of material that you are using for making this book cover will influence your method of transferring the design (for full instructions on transferring the design and backing see page 7). If you are using silk or a finer fabric trace the design, with a fine lead pencil, onto the fabric, neaten the raw edges, then back with fine poplin or lawn fabric to strengthen.

To embroider the Flowers

I have used *one strand of rayon thread* (approximately equal to *two threads of stranded cotton*) to embroider this book cover as rayon gives a nice sheen to the work and compliments the silk fabric it is worked on. There are a number of rayon and silk threads available, use whichever threads you prefer.

The crewel no. 8 needle is used with metallic thread. The crewel No. 9 or 10 is used for buttonhole, fishbone and single Brussels stitch. Single Brussels stitch can also be stitched using a tapestry No. 24 if preferred but the crewel needle goes through the material at the end of each row more easily. A tapestry No. 24 is also used for needlelace.

NEEDLE BOOK

PIN CUSHION

Book Cover

SCISSOR'S CASE
'ROSE' SIDE

SCISSOR'S CASE
'STRAWBERRY' SIDE

BUTTON BOX

KINGFISHER THIMBLE HOLDER

Petal Hussif

THREAD GUIDE

Thread	DMC rayon	Anchor stranded cotton	Au Ver a Soie D'Alger	Perlee
vermilion red	30498*	13	1026	681
olive green	30469*	1268	2136	
light leaf green	30472*	254	2142	
fawn	30738*	367	4222	
plum	33685*	70	3026	648
cranberry	33350*	78	3025	222
variegated turquoise/tan Dyepot D56 silk	91/105	1211/1218	1722,24/4513	
variegated apricot Dyepot D61 silk	3825	868	922	478
fine gold metallic thread plus fine red metallic thread				

apricot

vermillion

olive green

The book cover does not have to be worked in any particular order. However, you may find it easier if you couch on the heavy gold cord double heart shape first. Then work all the coloured embroidery filling in the leaves and petals. Next couch on the tendrils and round the edges of all the petals and leaves. Lastly sew on the beads. To complete, attach the embroidered cover to the book and then sew the heavy gold cord over the join.

THE CENTRAL DESIGN

Start and finish at the centre top. Use the heavy gold cord and couch it to the central double heart shaped design. Anchor the cord firmly at the base of the design. The cord crosses at the centre. For detailed information on couching and how to bring heavy cord through your material refer to page 14.

PLEASE NOTE

* DMC Rayon thread has been used. The numbers are the same as the stranded cottons except they have an additional '3' or '30' in front of the stranded cotton number.

LEAVES

All leaves are worked in fishbone stitch with the colours shown in the diagram given.

THE ROSE

The rose is created with three layers of petals worked in needlelace and a fourth layer of petals stitched onto the fabric. The petals worked directly onto the fabric are worked in buttonhole stitch using vermilion red thread. Note these petals are only worked where shown - the needlelace petals will cover the rest of the area.

The sepals, worked between each of the petals, are worked in fishbone stitch using olive green thread.

As the needlelace petals will be applied over the top of these petals and sepals (contrary to our general instruction) it is best to couch round the edge of both now using fine gold metallic thread.

The bottom and middle layer of needlelace petals are worked using variegated apricot thread, the top layer of needlelace is worked in vermilion red. All needlelace is worked using a tapestry No. 24 needle. Trace the outlines of the three layers of needlelace petals given, onto tracing paper and make the rose following the needlelace instructions given on page 18. For the foundation thread of the bottom two layers of needlelace use the variegated apricot thread used for the needlelace and couch with a matching apricot sewing cotton. For the foundation thread of the top layer of petals use the vermilion red thread used for the needlelace and couch with matching red sewing cotton.

LEAF KEY

⬚ *fawn thread*	▦ *olive green thread*
▨ *light leaf green thread*	▨ *variegated turquoise / tan thread*

On completion of the needlelace use fine light gold thread to buttonhole around the edges of the completed petals. Make up the rose following the instructions given on page 20.

CARNATION

The carnation is worked in single Brussels stitch throughout using two shades of thread. Starting at the base of the petal, work the three shaded petals in single Brussels stitch using plum thread. The other two petals are worked using cranberry thread.

The calyx is worked in single Brussels stitch using fine gold metallic thread, starting at the base, for detailed information on stitching a caylx refer to page 22.

COUCHING

For detailed information on couching refer to page 14.

The use of different cords is shown on the diagram facing.

The leaf stalks and little tendrils coming away from the main double heart design have been couched using medium gold cord.

With the embroidery of all the coloured petals and leaves complete, couch round the edge of every petal and leaf using fine gold metallic thread. When you are couching round the leaves, still using the same thread embroider the veins in straight stitches, refer to the diagram for additional detail.

The same heavy gold cord that was used to couch in the central design is also used for the first border which is couched on now. The second border is not couched until after the cover is applied to the backing.

Complete the carnation by sewing a 4 mm gold bead at the base of the calyx where indicated and the rose by sewing a 5 mm gold bead at its centre. A variety of different coloured beads have been sewn where indicated all over the cover.

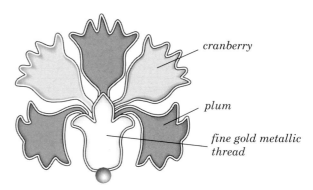

cranberry

plum

fine gold metallic thread

TO MAKE UP

Cut a piece of your main fabric and a piece of lining fabric 25 x 48 cm, (this includes seam allowances), press flat.

Now trim 2 cm off the lining fabric on each side. (Trimmed size 21 x 44 cm). This will make your seams much less bulky.

Place the lining fabric in the centre on the wrong side of your main fabric and turn the main fabric in 1 cm and press. Turn in again another 1 cm and press. Check that this fits your book. It should overlap the book edges by a fraction - say 2 mm.

Machine stitch the hem down on all four sides. (The lining is caught in this stitching.)

Wrap the cover around the book. Fold 6 cms at each end to the inside of the book. Stitch across the top and bottom by hand as invisibly as possible to join. This creates two 'pockets' for your book to slip into.

Now slip stitch the embroidered front in place and couch heavy gold cord over the seam. Tuck the beginning and endings of the heavy cord between the embroidered front piece and the book cover.

Your book cover is complete, just leave it in a very conspicuous position and wait for the compliments!

*start and
finish here*

Cords Key

⬭ *heavy gold cord*

⬭⬭⬭ *medium gold cord*

— *fine gold metalic thread*

— *red metallic thread*

*anchor firmly at the bottom where
the cord is turned back sharply on
itself to form the heart*

BUTTON BOX

(finished size of embroidery 18 x 10 cm)

Refer to the colour photograph on
page 54 for additional detail

Beautifully embroidered boxes have been much admired for
many centuries. Earlier needlewomen made them to store sewing
requisites, jewellery, writing materials or other special treasures.
This richly embroidered box top has been designed so that it can
easily be adjusted to fix box tops of a slightly different size. The
use of threads with a sheen, plus generous amounts of couched
gold cord and beads give this box a most sumptuous appearance.

YOU WILL NEED

- Wooden box with an 18 by 10 cm space for embroidery, refer
  to page 9 for notes on increasing or decreasing the size of this
  design
- 25 x 22 cm gold coloured satin
- .3 m of backing - lawn or poplin large enough to fit frame
- frame - large enough to fit whole design
- needlepunch to fit the size of the design - 18 x 10 cm.
- 1 m x 2 mm gold Russian Braid
- Three different thicknesses of gold metallic cord and thread:
  - 1 m x 2 mm *craft gold metallic* - referred to as 'heavy' cord
  - 0.5 m x 1 mm *crinkle gold metallic cord* - referred to as
  'medium' cord
  - *Fil light gold thread DM 282* - referred to as fine gold
  metallic thread
- Gutermann 968 or any good matching thread for couching on
  gold metallic threads
- Embroidery threads required listed separately with each
  flower
- Beads - numerous gold seed beads, 7 petite gold, 6 x 1 mm
  gold, 12 dark red seed, 6 Mill Hill Antique Cranberry seed
  03003, 16 Mill Hill Midnight Rainbow 00374 1 mm beads
- Stiff cardboard 18 - 10 cm
- UHU glue, or similar

DESIGN TO BE TRACED

Preparation

Before you can begin to stitch you must transfer the design onto the fabric. The type of material that you are using for the box top will influence your method of transferring the design (for full instructions on transferring the design see page 7). As I used satin I was able to trace the design directly on to it using a fine lead pencil. I then backed it with fine poplin or lawn fabric to strengthen. Put it in a frame large enough to take the complete design. For further information on backing and framing refer to page 7.

To embroider the Flowers

The flowers can be embroidered in whichever order you prefer. However the 'carnation' leaves need to be worked before the heavy cord is couched on - as the leaves actually go under the couched cord. I prefer to couch round each petal and leaf on the completion of all coloured thread embroidery. The instructions for sewing on beads are given with each flower but it is easier to stitch the beads and the needlelace butterfly wing on last as the threads tend to catch on these.

I have used *one strand of rayon thread* throughout as I like the sheen this gives the embroidery. *Two threads of stranded cotton* could be used instead of the rayon, plus there are many other silk and hand dyed threads that could be used most effectively - use the threads that you enjoy working with, or branch out and try something new.

All satin, stem, long and short, fishbone stitch and couching to be worked using a crewel No. 9 or 10 needle. This may also be the easiest needle to use when working single Brussels stitch as it goes through the material at the end of each row more smoothly. Alternatively you could use a tapestry needle No. 24. This is also used for working the needlelace.

Carnations

Threads	DMC rayon	Anchor stranded cotton	Au ver a soie D'Alger	Perlee
pink	33689*	74	3021	
dark pink	33687*	76	3024	631
light green	30368*	208	5023	
fine light metallic gold thread				

Starting at the centre fill the outer, pale pink petals, in satin stitch worked in pink thread.

The base petals are worked in single Brussels stitch starting at the base of the petal and using dark pink. Ignore the calyx when you stitch the base petals as the centre point of the calyx will be worked over the top of the base of these petals.

Starting at the base of the calyx, using fine light metallic gold thread fill the area with single Brussels stitch. Work the three points separately and stitch them over the top of the base petals, especially the centre point.

At the completion of all embroidery sew six dark red seed beads on the base petals.

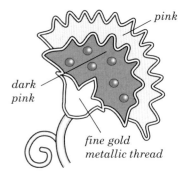

pink

dark pink

fine gold metallic thread

Honeysuckle

Threads	DMC rayon	Anchor stranded cotton	Au ver a soie D'Alger	Perlee
maroon	30814*	44	2926	
salmon pink	30352*	10	2643	
leaf green	30472*	254	2142	

The four lower petals and the centre top petal have been worked in satin stitch, starting at the centre using maroon.

The two top side petals have been worked in long and short stitch using salmon pink. The first row of stitches closely follows the outline of each petal.

At the completion of all embroidery sew a 1 mm gold bead at the centre of the honeysuckle.

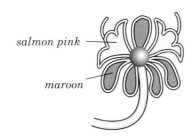

salmon pink

maroon

Rose

Threads	DMC rayon	Anchor stranded cotton	Au ver a soie D'Alger	Perlee
plum	33685*	70	3026	
warm gold	30676*	891	2611	

All the petals of the rose have been worked in padded satin stitch using plum thread. It is easier to get the stitches on the desired slant if the satin stitching is started in the centre of each petal.

The five small sepals have been worked in fishbone stitch using warm gold.

At the completion of all embroidery sew a 1 mm gold bead at the centre of the rose.

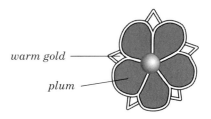

warm gold

plum

Handy Hints

For best results we recommend you stitch all the designs in the sequence given.

Please Note

* DMC Rayon thread has been used. The numbers are the same as the stranded cottons except they have an additional '3' or '30' in front of the stranded cotton number.

FUCHSIA

Threads	DMC rayon	Anchor stranded cotton	Au ver a soie D'Alger	Perlee
Pale salmon pink	30754*	868	2641	
red	30326*	42	945	
plum	33685*	70	3026	
olive green	30469*	268	2136	

Work the three top petals in fishbone stitch using pale salmon pink. The three lower petals have been worked in satin stitch using red. Start at the centre of each petal.

The fuchsia has a 1 mm gold bead sewn at the base of each flower. With plum thread work three straight stitches to form the stamen coming down from the fuchsia flower and sew a little gold seed bead at the end of each stamen.

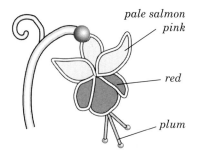

pale salmon pink

red

plum

BIRD

Threads	DMC rayon	Anchor stranded cotton	Au ver a soie D'Alger	Perlee
Dark tan	30435*	365	3825	
warm gold	30676*	891	2611	
maroon	30814*	44	2926	
dark blue	30336*	150	161	
fine light gold metallic thread				

The main body section of the bird is worked in single Brussels stitch using dark tan.

The wing is worked in three sections with the rows of stem stitch worked very closely together. The section closest to the body is worked using warm gold, the next section is worked in maroon, the outer section and the other wing is worked in dark blue.

The tail is also worked in stem stitch in three sections with the longest, outer section in warm gold, the middle section in maroon and the inner section in darkblue.

The crown is worked in single Brussels stitch using fine light gold metallic thread. With the same thread and straight stitches work the legs, feet, beak and 'v' shapes over the body of the bird. Refer to the diagram for additional detail.

Complete with a gold seed bead for the bird's eye.

fine light metallic gold thread

dark blue

maroon

warm gold

dark tan

dark blue

maroon

warm gold

Borage (blue flower)

Threads	DMC rayon	Anchor stranded cotton	Au ver a soie D'Alger	Perlee
light blue	33325*	140	4922	
mid blue	30322*	142	4923	
fine light gold metallic thread				

The petals are worked in fishbone stitch. Work the two back (shaded) petals first using mid blue, then stitch the three front petals using light blue.

The centre top petal is worked in three steps.

• First the petal is worked in fishbone stitch using light blue thread.

• Still using the same thread backstitch from the base of the petal to its tip along the left hand edge. These stitches will anchor the subsequent single Brussels stitch. Now work four rows of single Brussels stitch. This creates one side of the seed pocket. Repeat along the right hand side of the petal.

• Fill the pocket with eight Midnight Rainbow beads. Using fine metallic gold thread, couch around the edges of the pocket enclosing the beads.

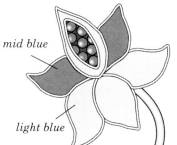

mid blue

light blue

Butterfly

Threads	DMC rayon	Anchor stranded cotton	Au ver a soie D'Alger	Perlee
Dark tan	30435*	365	3825	
maroon	30814*	44	2921	
pale salmon pink	30754*	868	2641	
dark blue	30336*	150	161	

The body of the butterfly is worked in satin stitch starting at the centre and using dark tan.

The butterfly's wing is worked in two parts with the back section embroidered in satin stitch directly onto the fabric. The section nearest to the body is stitched in maroon and the outer area is stitched in pale salmon pink. Refer to the diagram for placement of these colours.

The top section of the wing is worked in needlelace. (Refer to page 18 for full instructions on this technique.) Trace the outline from the pattern. The foundation thread is pale salmon pink and this is couched into position with sewing cotton of a matching colour. The wing filling is worked in single Brussels stitch started at the inner edge and using maroon. When you have stitched one third of the wing change to pale salmon pink to complete. Edge the wing in buttonhole stitch, using fine metallic gold thread with the stitches worked very closely together. This stiffens the wing and helps it to stand up.

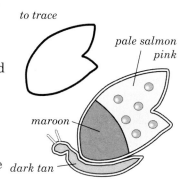

to trace

pale salmon pink

maroon

dark tan

LEAF KEY

leaf green
light green
olive green
dark blue
tan
maroon

Sew six Antique Cranberry seeds on the needlelace wing and then put the wing carefully to one side. It is sewn on with the beads at the completion of your embroidery.

LEAVES
All leaves are worked in fishbone stitch with the colours shown in the diagram given.

COUCHING AND BEADS

For detailed information on couching refer to page 14.

With the coloured thread embroidery complete couch fine gold metallic thread around all the petals and leaves. Work the veins on the leaves also. Refer to the diagrams for additional detail.

Thread a crewel No. 9 needle with the metallic thread and a crewel No. 10 with the sewing cotton to be used for couching and you will find that you can do this quite quickly. The honeysuckle stamen is one stitch couched down in a curve. When couching round the flowers remember to couch between the petals and also between the different colours on the wing and tail of the bird.

Couch the main design lines, the 'S' shapes into place using heavy gold cord, the small tendrils coming off the main 'S' lines are couched in medium gold cord.

TO COMPLETE

Sew a sprinkling of gold seed beads where indicated on the background fabric and sew the beads on the individual flowers. Refer to the instructions given with each flower.

TO MAKE UP

With your embroidery complete trim the *backing* fabric to the size of the box top embroidery space - 18 x 10 cms. Trim the satin back so that it *extends 2 cms beyond* the embroidery on each side. Take a piece of firm card 18 x 10 cm, lay a piece of needlepunch the same size over the card. (I use a strip of double sided Sellotape to hold the needlepunch in position.) Now lace your embroidery over the card.

Place laced embroidery into the space in the box top to check it is a good fit. Pin the Russian braid on the extreme edge of your embroidery and stitch in the centre of the braid (it is not couched) with the thread using for couching. Stitch so that the outside edge of the braid rests on the box and covers the join. Start at the corner, turning the braid under 6 mm. It is easier to stitch the braid in place off the box top, but keep checking it, by putting it in position on the box to make certain the Russian braid is in the correct place especially at the corners.

It helps to put a pin through the braid as you approach a corner. Care needs to be taken in stitching the braid round the corners nicely - it is easier to round the corners ever so slightly than to go really sharply round the corners. Finish by turning the braid under at the corner where you started, about 6 mm and continue stitching in place. An extra stitch or two may be required to hold the starting and finishing points of the braid together

Once you are satisfied all is complete, glue the embroidery into place with UHU or similar glue.

Now enjoy looking at and using your own beautiful box.

PETAL HUSSIF

(finished height 16 cm)

Refer to the colour photograph on the front cover and
page 56 for additional detail

Decorated with the richness so reminiscent of Elizabethan embroidery this delightful and most unusual hussif has been designed to give the illusion of an opening flower. The richly embroidered outer petals opening and closing as flowers do. The inner bag gives the impression of more petals and the central golden lining reminds you of golden, pollen bearing stamens. The outer petals each feature one flower contained within a frame of heavy gold cord. The bag is opened by loosening the red cord allowing the petals to fall open revealing an embroidered pocket on the inside of each petal. Just the place to put needles, pins, and the other little bits and pieces so necessary to an embroiderer. Stitched in a variety of soft shades the Petal Hussif is beautiful open or closed.

The rich appearance of this bag could make it an heirloom piece just for show or as a gift for a someone very special, but it is strongly constructed to serve well for its practical purpose. The small pockets on the inner petals and the roomy inner drawstring bag make it a useful carryall for your current work. With this hussif you could carry your stitching anywhere!

YOU WILL NEED

- 25 cm of Brittney (maroon) red
- 50 cm of red (maroon) Pongee material for backing
- 60 cm of green imitation linen
- 25 cm of Pongee (green) or lining material
- 60 cm of gold satin
- 25 cm of heavy vylene
- Crewel No.s 8, 9, and 10, Tapestry No. 24
- Gutermann 968 or any good matching thread for couching on gold metallic threads

DESIGNS TO BE TRACED
position carefully on fabric

- Sewing thread to match the main fabrics
- 10 cm embroidery frame for working the inner pockets
- 18 cm embroidery frame for working the outer petals - this fits the entire design
- 20 cm of 5 mm gold metallic ribbon, used to hold the pin wheel together
- 60 cm of ribbon to match red (maroon) Brittney
- felt for raised work petals say 10 cm square
- A complete list of embroidery threads used is given in the Thread Guide. These are given as a guide only, feel free to substitute for your own favourite or preferred threads
- 2 m x 2 mm gold fabric cord for the drawstring of the inner bag
- 1 m x 2mm red fabric cord for the drawstring of the petals
- Three different thicknesses of gold metallic cord and thread:
  - 4 m x 2mm *craft gold metallic* - referred to as 'heavy' cord
  - 3 m x 1 mm *crinkle gold metallic cord* - referred to as 'medium' cord
  - *Fil light gold thread DM 282* - referred to as fine gold metallic thread
- card or plastic from an empty ice cream container
- 1.5 cm gold bead, 10 x 3 mm gold beads, 13 x 2 mm gold beads, plus gold petite beads

This hussif has five petals made from maroon Brittney linen with a large embroidered motif on the outside of each petal and a smaller embroidered flower on the inside of each petal, stitched on the pocket. The petals are then stitched to the inner bag. The inner drawstring bag is made from two layers of fabric, green linen on the outside and gold satin on the inside, to resemble the centre of a flower. The inner bag is drawn up with gold cord and the petals are drawn up separately with matching maroon coloured cord.

TO TRANSFER THE DESIGNS

The type of material that you are using will influence your method of transferring the designs for this hussif. Different ways of transferring the designs are given on page 7. Bearing in mind whichever method you choose to use, transfer the outline and flower shapes to your material at the appropriate time. If tracing (I use a light box and then even this 'Brittney' can be seen through) do so before you have put the material in the frame. If using templates the shapes are transferred when the material is in the frame.

PREPARATION

Make a template of the petal shape shown in fig. 1. Trace the outline, glue onto a piece of card and then cut out.

Now use this template to cut out **ten** shapes from the heavy vylene exactly the same size as the template. When the shapes have been cut out in vylene, trim 6 mm from the bottom edge of each vylene shape (this will reduce the bulk in construction at the base of the hussif).

Using the same template, cut out **ten** shapes from the maroon material *1 cm larger on the sides and tip, but 3 cms longer at the base*. (This is to enable adjustments to be made when assembling the hussif.) Neaten the edges to prevent fraying.

Put five pieces of vylene and five pieces of material to one side, these are to be used for the backs of the petals. The other five pieces of vylene and material are used for the front of each petal.

If you are going to trace the designs onto the fabric now is the time to do it. To ensure the correct placement of the designs on your petal shaped fabric you may find it easier if you create another template. To do this trace round the outside edge of the petal, then trace the outer edge of the design (fig. 1). Glue this to

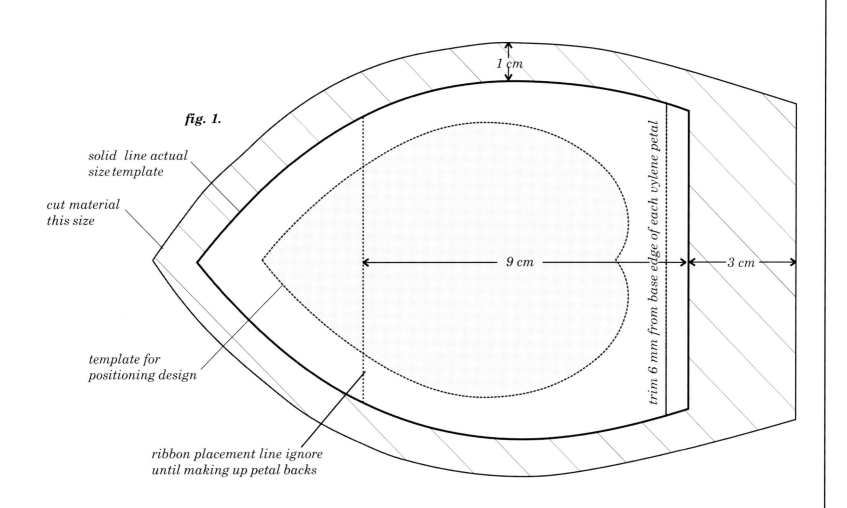

fig. 1.

solid line actual
size template

cut material
this size

template for
positioning design

ribbon placement line ignore
until making up petal backs

1 cm

9 cm

3 cm

trim 6 mm from base edge of each vylene petal

a piece of card then cut out the central area. Now rest this template on top of your fabric, position the flower design ready for tracing within this shape and your embroidery will be perfectly positioned. Remember to tack the outside petal edge also. This will be invaluable later when positioning the vylene on the fabric petal.

Stretch the red backing material onto an 18 cm hoop, this is large enough to fit the whole petal design, then tack the petal onto the stretched backing as evenly as possible. You are now ready to embroider the flowers.

THE PETALS
TO EMBROIDER THE FLOWERS

I have used *one strand of rayon thread* (approximately equal to *two threads of stranded cotton*) to embroider this hussif as rayon gives a nice sheen to the work and compliments the fabric it is worked on. There are a number of rayon and silk threads available to use, and if you have never used them before, this could be the ideal time to start. Feel free to use whichever threads you prefer.

The crewel no. 8 needle is used with metallic thread. The crewel No. 9 or 10 is used for buttonhole, closed stem, satin, fishbone and single Brussels stitch in raised work. Single Brussels stitch can also be stitched using a tapestry No. 24 if preferred but the crewel needle goes through the material at the end of each row more easily.

COUCHING

There is extensive use of different weights of couched gold cord and thread on the embroidery on the outside of each petal. Contrary to my other projects I couched the heavy gold cord, which gives the outside design line and main stems, in position first on these petals. This gave me a frame to work within. I then did the raised work, followed by the fine embroidery.

On completion of the embroidery I did the remaining couching required, applying medium gold cord for the tendrils and fine gold metallic thread around and between each of the petals, leaves and buds. To couch the fine metallic thread quickly I thread a crewel No. 8 needle with the metallic thread and a crewel No. 10 with the sewing cotton to be used for couching and you will find that you can do this quite quickly. I applied the beads last of all. The gold cord couched around the outside of each petal is applied *after* the front and back petals have been joined together. For detailed information on couching refer to page 14.

HANDY HINT

For best results we recommend that you stitch each of the designs in the sequence given.

PLEASE NOTE

Throughout the text

* = DMC Rayon thread has been used. The numbers are the same as the stranded cottons except they have an additional '3' or '30' in front of the stranded cotton number.

ROSE

Thread	DMC rayon	Anchor stranded cotton	Au Ver a Soie D'Alger	Perlee
deep pink	33687*	76	3024	631
medium green	30367*	210	1835	

heavy and medium gold cord and fine gold metallic thread

Cut felt templates for the five rose petals. These are stitched in 'raised work' using deep pink throughout. The sepals showing between the petals have been worked in straight stitches using medium green.

The small leaves have been worked in fishbone stitch also using medium green.

The buds are worked in straight stitches using deep pink for the tip and medium green for the base of the bud.

Heavy and medium gold cord and fine gold thread have been used for couching, refer to the diagram for their placement. Complete the rose by sewing a gold flat bead with a gold seed bead at the centre, 2 x 3 mm and 3 x 2 mm gold beads have been sewn where indicated. Petite gold beads have been sewn over the background where indicated.

HANDY HINT
Instructions for doing raised work petals are given on page 21.

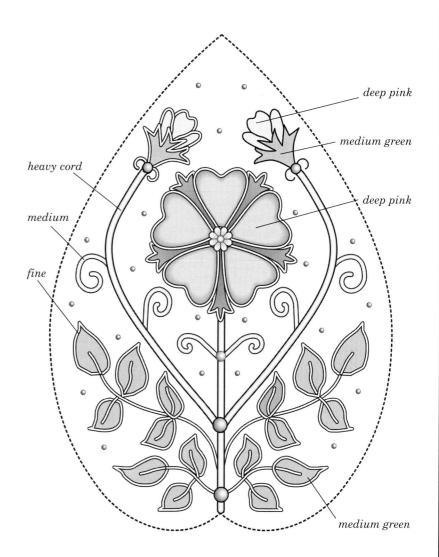

deep pink

medium green

heavy cord

deep pink

medium

fine

medium green

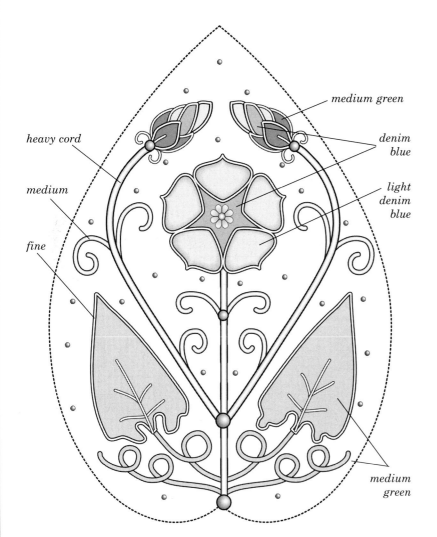

heavy cord

medium

fine

medium green

denim blue

light denim blue

medium green

Convolvulus

Thread	DMC rayon	Anchor stranded cotton	Au Ver a Soie D'Alger	Perlee
light denim blue	30932*	1033	4912	016
denim blue	30931*	1034	4913	
medium green	30367*	210	1835	
heavy and medium gold cord and fine gold metallic thread				

Cut felt templates of the five large petals, these are stitched in 'raised work' using light denim blue throughout.

The centre of the convolvulus and the buds above the main flower are worked in denim blue thread in satin stitch. The leaves beneath the buds are worked in medium green also in satin stitch.

The two large leaves at the base have been worked in fishbone stitch using medium green. The stem is also medium green but all the threads have been used and it has been couched in place.

Heavy and medium gold cord and fine gold thread have been used for couching, refer to the diagram for their placement. Complete the convolvulus by sewing a gold flat bead with a gold seed bead at the centre, 2 x 3 mm and 1 x 2 mm gold beads have been sewn where indicated. Petite gold beads have been sewn over the background. Refer to the diagram for their placement.

DAFFODIL

Thread	DMC rayon	Anchor stranded cotton	Au Ver a Soie D'Alger	Perlee
golden yellow	30744*	305	2532	674
dark golden yellow	33820*	306	2533	
leaf green	30472	254	2142	
heavy and medium gold cord and fine gold metallic thread				

Cut felt templates for the six large petals, these are stitched in 'raised work' using golden yellow throughout.

The centre of the daffodil has been worked in satin stitch using dark golden yellow. To bring the centre forward two rows of detached buttonhole stitch have been worked around the outside edge of the centre, the first using dark golden yellow thread and the second row worked using fine gold metallic thread.

The two buds have been worked in satin stitch with the central area stitched in golden yellow and the outer petals stitched in dark golden yellow.

The four tapering leaves at the base have been worked in closed stem stitch using leaf green.

Heavy and medium gold cord and fine gold thread have been used for couching, refer to the diagram for their placement. Complete the daffodil by sewing a gold seed bead at the centre, 2 x 3 mm and 3 x 2 mm gold beads have been sewn where indicated. Petite gold beads have been sewn over the background. Refer to the diagram for their placement.

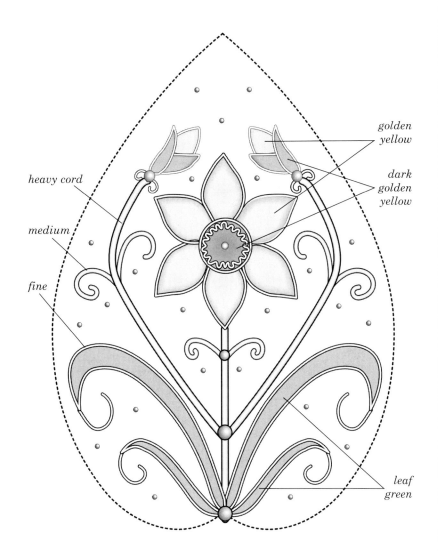

golden yellow

dark golden yellow

heavy cord

medium

fine

leaf green

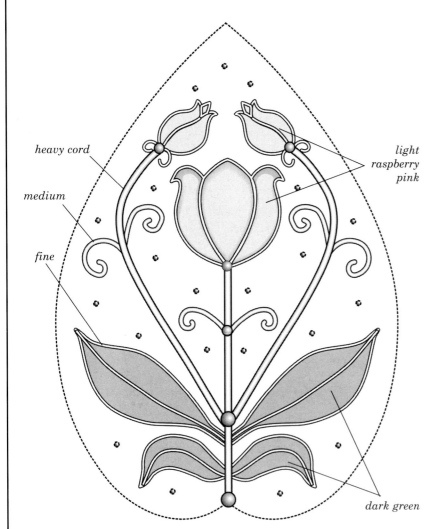

heavy cord

medium

fine

light
raspberry
pink

dark green

TULIP

Thread	DMC rayon	Anchor stranded cotton	Au Ver a Soie D'Alger	Perlee
light raspberry pink	33689*	74	3031	
dark green	30895*	1044	1846	
heavy and medium gold cord and fine gold metallic thread				

Cut felt templates for the three large petals, these are stitched in 'raised work' using light raspberry pink throughout. Still using the same thread stitch the two buds in satin stitch.

The leaves at the base of the tulip are worked in fishbone stitch using dark green.

Heavy and medium gold cord and fine gold thread have been used for couching, refer to the diagram for their placement. Complete the tulip by sewing 2 x 3 mm and 4 x 2 mm gold beads where indicated. Petite gold beads have been sewn over the background. Refer to the diagram for their placement.

HANDY HINT
If you are finding it hard to trace a design on dark fabric darken the outline of the design to be traced or transfer it with dressmakers carbon.

Iris

Thread	DMC rayon	Anchor stranded cotton	Au Ver a Soie D'Alger	Perlee
mid blue	30322*	142	4923	
light blue	33325*	140	4922	417
golden yellow	30744*	305	2532	
fawn	30738*	372	4222	
light green	30368*	208	5023	

heavy and medium gold cord and fine gold metallic thread

Cut felt templates for the two lower petals in the main flower and the centre top petal these are all stitched in 'raised work' using light blue for the two lower petals and mid blue for the centre top petal.

The two top side petals are stitched in satin stitch using mid blue. The calyx showing at each side beneath the three upper petals and in centre front is stitched in satin stitch using golden yellow.

The buds are worked in satin stitch with the base (calyx) stitched in fawn with light blue in the centre and mid blue at the top.

The leaves at the base of the tulip are worked in closed stem stitch using light green.

Heavy and medium gold cord and fine gold thread have been used for couching, refer to the diagram for their placement. Complete the tulip by sewing 2 x 3 mm and 2 x 2 mm gold beads where indicated. Petite gold beads have been sewn over the background. Refer to the diagram for their placement.

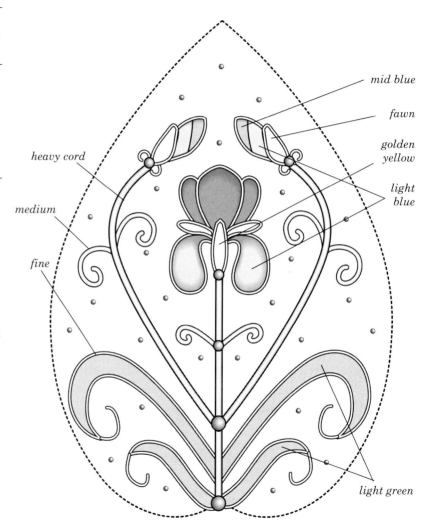

Making the front petals

With all five petals embroidered, trim the backing to the finished size of the petal. Lay the petal out flat with the wrong side facing you. Place the vylene carefully inside the tacked outline of the petals. The vylene will be 6 mm short of the base tacked outline. (This was trimmed earlier to reduced bulk when constructing the hussif.)

Turn the side edges of the petal over the top of the vylene. Stitch the petal onto the vylene *down each side, **not** across the bottom,* making certain that the stitches do not go through to the front. A few nicks on the curves will help to keep the turning from becoming bulky. Take care to ensure that a nice point is formed. Put the five petals carefully to one side until the back of each petal is made.

To make the Pockets
finished size 7 cm square

Cut five 9 cm square pieces of fabric from the green linen. This includes a 1 cm seam allowance on all sides. Cut five 9 x 12 cm lining pieces from the gold satin. Neaten all edges.

There are five different pocket designs, trace one design onto each square of green linen positioning the flower with the base of the stem 2 cms from the raw edge of the material. Stretch the backing onto a 10 cm hoop. Tack a green pocket top to the backing and embroider each pocket.

Pocket

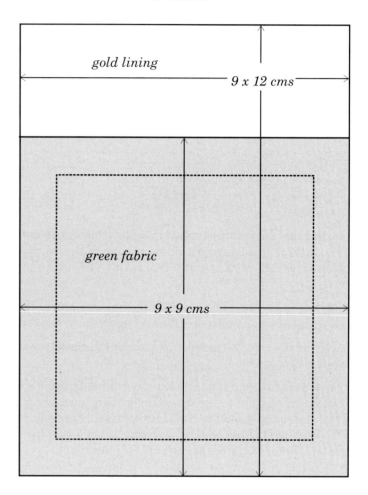

gold lining

9 x 12 cms

green fabric

9 x 9 cms

PRIMROSE

Thread	DMC rayon	Anchor stranded cotton	Au Ver a Soie D'Alger	Perlee
golden yellow	30744*	305	2532	
dark golden yellow	33820*	306	2533	
olive green	30469*	268	2136	
medium gold cord and fine gold metallic thread				

The primrose has been worked in satin stitch with dark golden yellow at the centre and golden yellow on the outer edges. The leaves have been worked in fishbone stitch using olive green.

A gold seed bead has been sewn in the centre to complete the flower. Medium gold cord has been couched in place for the stem and fine gold thread has been couched around the petals and leaves. Refer to the diagram for their placement.

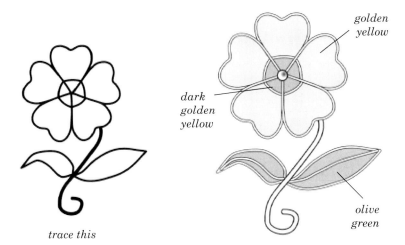

golden yellow

dark golden yellow

olive green

trace this

NARCISSUS

Thread	DMC rayon	Anchor stranded cotton	Au Ver a Soie D'Alger	Perlee
creamy white	30746*	275	2541	
warm gold	30676*	891	2611	
dark gold	30976*	308	2546	
leaf green	30472*	254	2142	
medium cord and fine gold metallic thread				

The six petals have been worked in fishbone stitch using creamy white thread. The centre has been satin stitched in warm gold with one row of whipped chain stitch worked in dark gold around the outer edge of the centre. The leaves have been worked in closed stem stitch using leaf green.

Medium gold cord has been couched in place for the stem and fine gold thread has been couched around the petals and leaves giving a delicate edging. Refer to the diagram for their placement.

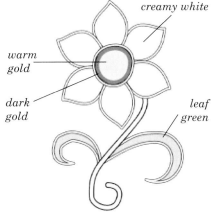

creamy white

warm gold

dark gold

leaf green

trace this

Columbine

Thread	DMC rayon	Anchor stranded cotton	Au Ver a Soie D'Alger	Perlee
cranberry	33350*	78	3025	
light cranberry	33733*	76	3022	
light green	30368*	208	5023	
medium gold cord, fine gold metallic thread				

The four top petals have been worked in fishbone stitch using cranberry. The three lower petals have been satin stitched using light cranberry with the calyx at the very top worked in satin stitch also using cranberry. The leaves have been worked in fishbone stitch using light green.

Medium gold cord has been used for the stem and fine gold thread has been couched around the petals to separate the petals and highlight the columbine.
Refer to the diagram for their placement.

trace this

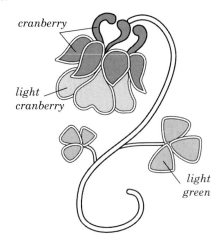

cranberry

light cranberry

light green

Love in the Mist

Thread	DMC rayon	Anchor stranded cotton	Au Ver a Soie D'Alger	Perlee
mid blue	30322*	131	4912	
light blue	33325*	140	4922	
light green	30368*	208	5023	
medium gold cord, fine gold metallic thread				

The petals and centre are all worked in satin stitch. The eight mid blue petals are worked first to ensure that a nice shaped petal is achieved, then the centre is worked, still in the mid blue. The alternating petals are worked in light blue.

The leaves are worked in whipped back stitch using light green thread.

Medium gold cord has been couched in place for the stem. Fine gold thread has been couched around the petals and leaves and used to work extra straight stitches to highlight the flower. Refer to the diagram for their placement.

trace this

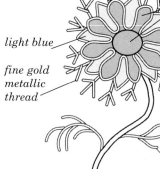

mid blue

light blue

fine gold metallic thread

light green

PANSY

Thread	DMC rayon	Anchor stranded cotton	Au Ver a Soie D'Alger	Perlee
maroon	30814*	44	2926	
red	30326*	42	945	
medium green	30367*	210	1835	
medium gold cord, fine gold metallic thread				

The petals are all worked in satin stitch with the two upper petals worked in maroon and the lower three worked in red.

The leaves are worked in fishbone stitch using medium green thread.

A gold seed bead has been placed in the centre of the pansy. Medium gold cord has been couched in place for the stem. Fine gold thread has been couched around the petals and leaves and used for some extra straight stitches on the lower petals. Refer to the diagram for their use.

trace this

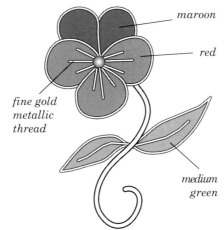

maroon

red

fine gold metallic thread

medium green

THE PETAL BACKS

(using the five pieces of vylene and material put to one side earlier)

Tack the outer edge of the petal on the five fabric pieces.

Trace from fig. 1 the ribbon position line on to each of the five pieces of vylene. Pin the maroon ribbon across the vylene petal with the top edge of the ribbon on this line. The ribbon should extend beyond the petal at least 1 cm on each side. Machine stitch close to the top and bottom edges of the ribbon, making a gusset for the red cord to go through. *Stop sewing 1.5 cm from each edge (fig. 2).*

Lay the maroon material petal out flat and put the vylene inside the tacked outline of the petal. The maroon ribbon will be facing you. (The vylene will be 6 mm short of the base tacked outline - this was trimmed earlier to reduced bulk when constructing the hussif.)

Stitch the fabric onto the vylene making certain that the stitches do not go through to the front, trim and nick to reduce bulk. When you come to the ribbon, stitch the ribbon by hand onto the turned back material along the top and bottom edge to join up with the machine sewing. The ends of the ribbon should be facing out so that they do not get pulled out with the cord. These ends will be hidden when you put the petal fronts and backs together.

POCKET CONSTRUCTION

Place the right side of the gold lining and the embroidered pieces together with the extra length of the gold material at the top. Sew together down each side and across the bottom. Trim corners and turn to right side. Press edges, *do not* iron over the embroidery.

Turn under the raw edge of the gold material so that you create an 8 mm edging on the top edge of the green material, slip stitch in place.

Position the pocket on the maroon fabric so that the top of the

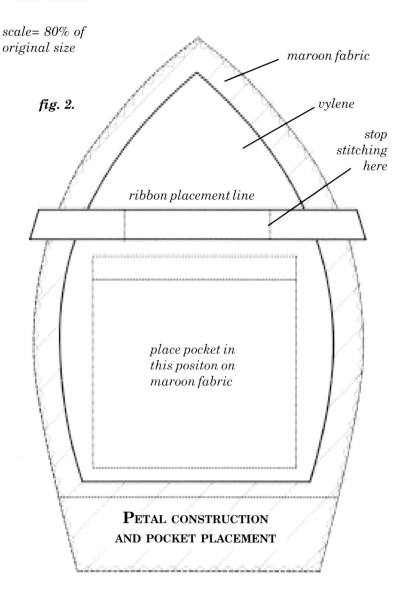

scale= 80% of original size

fig. 2.

maroon fabric

vylene

stop stitching here

ribbon placement line

place pocket in this positon on maroon fabric

PETAL CONSTRUCTION AND POCKET PLACEMENT

pocket is just below the bottom edge of the ribbon sewn onto the vylene (fig. 2). Pin, then machine stitch down the sides and across the bottom. Leave the 8 mm turn back unstitched. This allows easier access to the contents of the pockets.

Couch medium gold cord over the machine stitching and the join between the green and gold fabric, covering your slip stitches. The ends can be stitched down at the back of the pocket.

COMPLETING THE PETALS

Pin the petal backs and fronts together right sides out matching all the way round. Ladder stitch together invisibly leaving the gusset for the ribbon open. To cover the join, couch heavy gold cord all the way round the edge of the petal, including the extra 3 cms at the base of the petal. When you come to the opening for the gusset couch the gold cord on the outer petal. Leave couched gold cord ends free as these will be hidden in the construction. Put the five completed petals to one side.

DRAWSTRING BAG

Cut a 50 cms diameter circle from the green fabric. Mark the centre of the circle clearly. On the right side measure 4 cms in from the edge and mark a circle with a dressmakers pencil (for stitching the cord gusset). Mark a second circle 1 cm in from the first (fig. 3).

Trace round the pentagonal shape (fig. 4), cut out a template and on the right side of the green fabric draw round the pentagonal template. Make sure that the template is placed exactly in the centre. Line the centre of the pentagon with the centre of the circle by putting a pin through both and *mark clearly*.

Within the pentagonal shape, mark and cut a 4 x 4 cm cross in the centre of the area, The cross allows for turning to the right side when the green and gold circles have been stitched together and will be hidden.

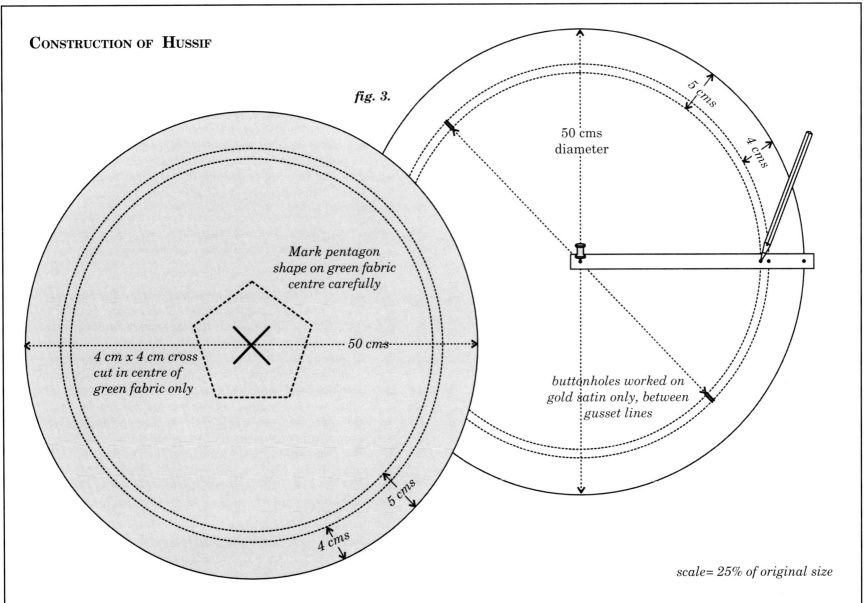

CONSTRUCTION OF HUSSIF

fig. 3.

Mark pentagon shape on green fabric centre carefully

4 cm x 4 cm cross cut in centre of green fabric only

50 cms

5 cms

4 cms

50 cms diameter

5 cms

4 cms

buttonholes worked on gold satin only, between gusset lines

scale= 25% of original size

fig. 4.

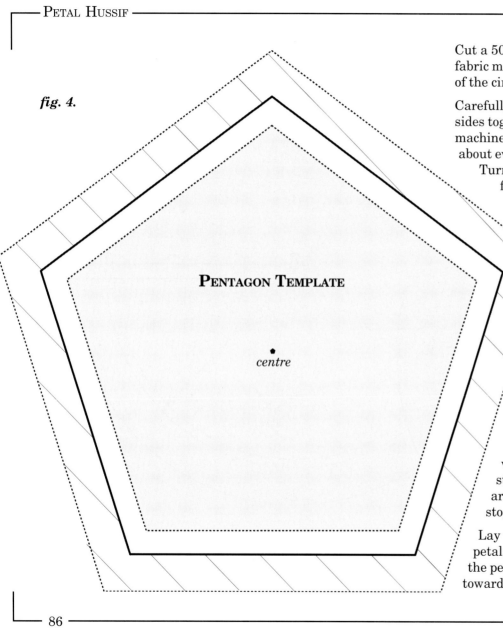

PENTAGON TEMPLATE

• centre

Cut a 50 cm diameter circle from the gold satin. As for the green fabric mark gusset lines then stitch a 1 cm buttonhole each side of the circle in the centre of the gusset lines (fig. 3).

Carefully pin the gold satin and green linen circles with right sides together 6 mm in from the edge all the way round and machine stitch together. Neaten the edge, then nick the curve about every 15 cms so that the circle will lie flat when turned. Turn the joined fabric circle back to the right side taking the fabric through the 4 cm cross that was cut in the centre of the green linen. Press carefully.

Now machine stitch on the two marked gusset lines. The two buttonholes should be in the centre of the 1 cm gusset lines.

To Assemble

Using the template already cut of the base pentagon cut the shape out in vylene, cut the vylene shape exactly the same size as the template. Cut a pentagon from plastic, then *trim 6 mm* from each side. Cut a pentagon from the maroon fabric *adding* an extra 1 cm for a seam allowance. Neaten the edges. Using double sided Sellotape or glue stick the plastic template to the centre of the vylene template then cover this with the maroon fabric once again turning the edges of the maroon fabric over the vylene and stitching the fabric to the vylene so that the stitches do not show on the right side. Machine stitch around the pentagon right beside the edge of the plastic to stop any movement. (A zipper foot may be useful).

Lay the circle, green side up, on a flat surface. Position the petals, one on each side of the pentagon with the base line of the petal on the pentagon line and the extra 3 cm extending in towards the centre.

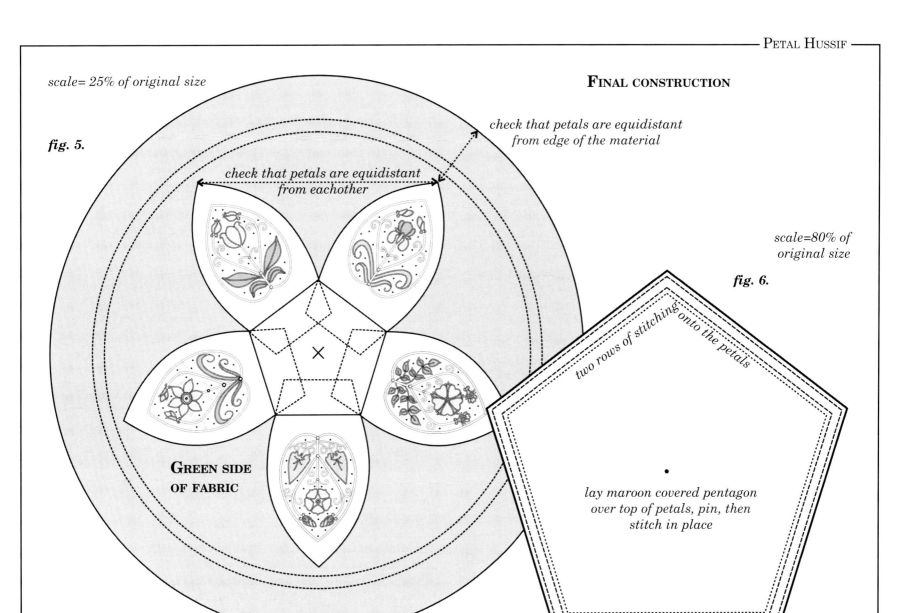

scale= 25% of original size

FINAL CONSTRUCTION

fig. 5.

check that petals are equidistant from edge of the material

check that petals are equidistant from eachother

scale=80% of original size

fig. 6.

GREEN SIDE OF FABRIC

two rows of stitching onto the petals

lay maroon covered pentagon over top of petals, pin, then stitch in place

Check that the tips of the petals are equidistant from each other and from the outer edge of the material circle (fig. 5). The base of the petals should meet at the corners, if they overlap a little it will not matter. This is where the extra length in the petals comes in handy for a little re-positioning if required.

Pin the petals in place. Lay the maroon covered pentagon base over the top of the petals. When you are happy that everything is positioned correctly, pin, then stitch in place. Machine stitch twice around the pentagon, the first time right on the edge of the material and the second about 6 mm inside the first line. (Just beside the plastic template in the base) fig. 6.

Cut the 2 metres of gold cord in half and thread one length through the gusset and back out the same buttonhole that it entered, tie ends together. Thread the other half through the other buttonhole and tie ends. Pull in opposite directions to close.

Thread the red cord through the petals, thread both ends through a large gold bead and tie. Make a tassel using stranded gold metallic thread and attach over the top of the knotted thread ends.

HANDY HINT

Check that the pin wheel fits into the pocket as you are working on it. It must not get too wide or fat.

ACCESSORIES

There are numerous items that the embroiderer likes to have to hand that can be placed in the little pockets on the inside of each petal, from tape measures to sewing wax and thimbles. We have instructions here for two very basic items that are always needed, a Pin Cushion Wheel and a Needle Book.

PIN CUSHION WHEEL

Cut a 5 cm diameter circle template. Use this to cut two circles of plastic or stiff card and two circles from the main green fabric remembering to add an extra 1 cm all round for the seam allowance.

The front of the pin wheel has a butterfly stitched in the centre. Trace the butterfly onto the green fabric, stretch backing material over a 10 cm hoop and tack on the main fabric ready to embroider.

BUTTERFLY

Thread	DMC rayon	Anchor stranded cotton	Au Ver a Soie D'Alger	Perlee
fuchsia pink	33608*	85	3032	
dark fuchsia pink	33607*	87	3045	
plum	33685*	70	3026	
slate blue	30930*	1035	1715	
fine gold metallic thread				

The wings have been worked in satin stitch with the outer wing area stitched first in fuchsia pink, and the inner wing area stitched in dark fuchsia pink. The two spots, one on each wing have been worked in plum in satin stitch.

The body has been worked in whipped chain stitch using slate blue thread.

Fine gold thread has been couched around the wings and body of the butterfly and also used to create the antennae. To complete a French knot has been worked in the same thread at the end of each antenna. Refer to the diagram for the placement of the fine gold thread.

When the embroidery is completed work a running stitch just in from the edge of the fabric to gather the circle up. Lay a circle of vylene, then the plastic or card circle inside the fabric, pull the running thread tightly and fasten off. Trim as necessary and lace across the back to hold in place securely. Couch medium gold cord round the edge. Repeat for the back side but embroider your initials and date in place of the butterfly.

Stitch the 5 mm gold metallic ribbon about 6 mm *inside* the edge at the back of each circle, poke in a little unspun wool or something similar for stuffing, then turn under the ribbon ends and join neatly. Put pins through ribbon round edge and place in one of the petal pockets.

NEEDLE BOOK

Cut a piece of vylene 10 cm x 5.5 cm.

Cut a piece each of gold and green fabric 12 x 7.5 cm. Neaten edges.

Trace the bee onto the centre right hand side of the green front cover. Stretch the backing material onto a 10 cm hoop, tack the green fabric in position and embroider the bee.

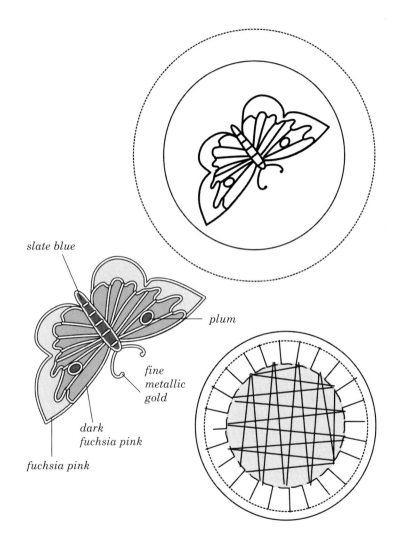

slate blue

plum

fine metallic gold

dark fuchsia pink

fuchsia pink

BEE

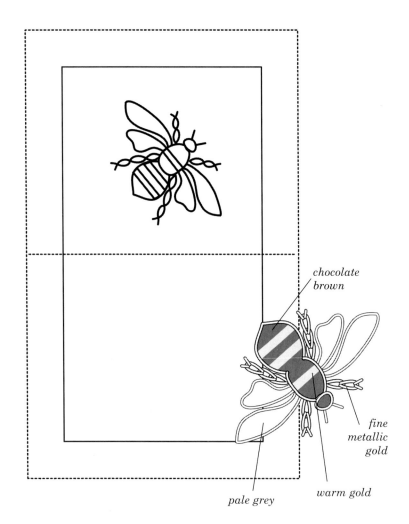

chocolate brown

fine metallic gold

warm gold

pale grey

Thread	DMC rayon	Anchor stranded cotton	Au Ver a Soie D'Alger	Perlee
chocolate brown	30898*	381	4143	
warm gold	30676*	891	2611	
pale grey	30762*	234	3441	
fine gold metallic thread				

The bee's body has been worked in satin stitch in chocolate brown and warm gold stripes with pale grey wings. Fine gold thread has been used to work the legs in chain stitch and it has also been couched around the wings and body of the bee and at the head.

When completed, place the vylene on the wrong side of the green fabric, turn in the edges and stitch to the vylene so that the stitches do not show on the right side. Trim corners to make them neat. Slip stitch gold lining right side out to the green cover positioning it about 3 mm inside the edge of the needle book on all sides. Press (not the embroidery) then couch gold crinkle cord all round the edge.

To make the needlebook pages cut two pieces of flannel approx 7 x 4 cm, neaten edges then sew to the gold lining at the centre of the cover. Couch medium gold cord over the inside centre crease tucking the ends of the cord under the flannel pages. To complete sew a 12mm gold bead on the back cover and make a buttonhole loop on the edge of the front cover to catch over it.

KINGFISHER THIMBLE HOLDER

Three dimensional embroideries were popular in the sixteenth and early part of the seventeenth centuries. They were often made by young girls after they had completed first their Sampler and then their casket. Two thimble holders shaped like birds have survived to this day and are held in museum collections, one at the Burrell Collection in Glasgow, the other at the Victoria and Albert, in London.

The revival of interest in three dimensional embroidery and the popularity of thimble collections make this Kingfisher Thimble Holder a very special way to store your favourite thimble and to serve as a decoration on your chair side table as you stitch.

I designed this Kingfisher in the 'style' of the bird in the Burrell Collection. It is about the same size but stitched a little differently, using different materials and modern threads. It is a twentieth century version, ready for use today. I have given the pattern, many diagrams and clear easy-to-follow instructions so that you can create your own Kingfisher Thimble Holder. I have given the thread colours and number of strands I used but these are a guide only, feel free to experiment, make your bird a different colour or experiment with the many hand-dyed threads for a different effect again. The scope for variety here is unlimited, just have fun making your own bird.

REQUIREMENTS

- 1 x 50 gram packet of Du-kit modelling clay for body (blue or flesh coloured)
- 15 cms of stiff wire (washing line grade) for legs and beak
- 25 cm square of turquoise satin, silk or some other fine material to be used for the pocket lining. This fabric will be seen so must match your threads well.
- 1 m of 10 mm turquoise rayon or other fine ribbon to match the satin or silk used for the pocket lining. This ribbon will also be seen.

(finished size approximately 14 x 7 cm)

Refer to the colour photograph on page 55 for additional detail

- 30 cm square of fine, strong material for the pocket top and base for the tail feathers - I used a closely woven heavy silk but a fine cotton or poplin could be used as it will not be seen.
- 50 cm of 1 mm cord to tone with pocket and bird - I used a dark green
- medium grade vylene (to cover small frame to work the feathers on)
- Crewel Needle No. 9, sewing needle, tapestry needle No. 24
- 2 small black sequins and 2 gold seed beads for eyes
- small embroidery hoop
- glue

THREADS

Marlitt*	056	dark Pacific turquoise
Marlitt*	105	Pacific turquoise
DMC Rayon*	30995	dark glacier turquoise
DMC Rayon*	30996	glacier turquoise
DMC Rayon*	33814	lagoon green
DMC Rayon*	30959	dark ice green
DMC Rayon*	30964	ice green
DMC Rayon	30738	fawn
DMC Stranded Cotton	934	very dark olive green
DMC Perle No. 5	738	fawn
DMC Metallic Antique Gold	273	
Sewing cotton Gutermann	870	dark turquoise
black sewing cotton		

* threads used for feathers

CONSTRUCTION OF THE BODY
BODY

The body is made from one whole 50 gram packet of Du-kit modelling clay with a tiny scrap put to one side for the beak. Du-kit is easy to mould, it softens as you work it with the warmth of your hands. While you are moulding the clay you may find the colour comes off on your hands, do not worry about this as once it is baked the colour is set.

Mould the bird to the shape and size shown in fig. 1 - but remember every bird will be different, just as they were in the seventeenth century. This will add to the individual charm of each bird.

After you have moulded your bird to a pleasing shape there are a number of things to do *before* the clay can be baked. We give detailed instructions on fig. 2 for the measurements of the bird, placement of cord holes, legs, beak etc. Mark the position of all these before actually making the holes and inserting the wire. Each bird will be different so just use these measurements as a guide and do remember to allow for your bird's individual differences.

CORD HOLES

Make a hole (approx 3 mm in diameter - a 3 mm knitting needle or a shish kebab stick will do the job nicely) through the body from just below the back of the bird's head, (4 cms from the tip of the head to the hole) to the front of the chest (3 cms from the beak to the hole in the chest) refer to fig. 2 for additional detail. This is for the cord used to tighten the little thimble pocket, to go through.

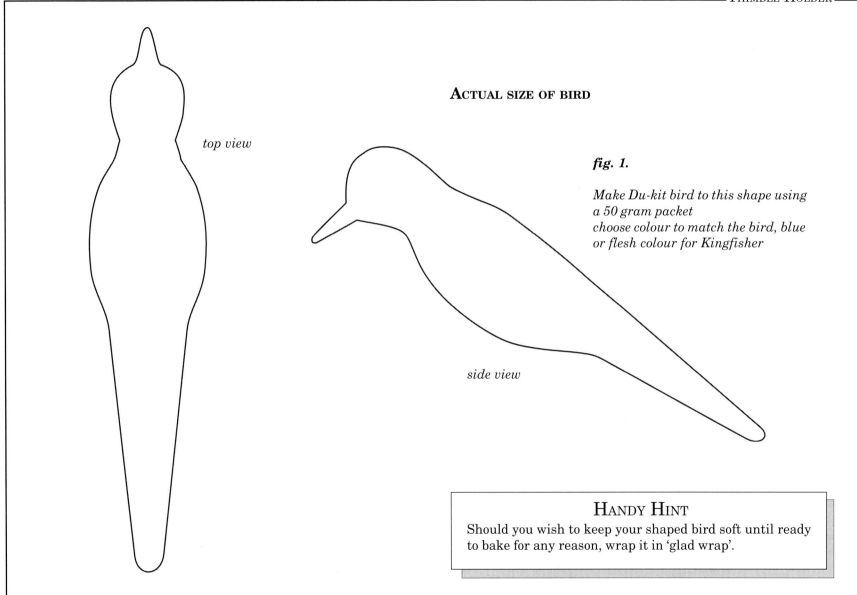

top view

ACTUAL SIZE OF BIRD

fig. 1.

Make Du-kit bird to this shape using a 50 gram packet
choose colour to match the bird, blue or flesh colour for Kingfisher

side view

HANDY HINT

Should you wish to keep your shaped bird soft until ready to bake for any reason, wrap it in 'glad wrap'.

MEASUREMENTS

HEAD

6.5 cm circumference round head

BEAK

1 beak - 2.5 cm wire, 1 cm in head, 1.5 cm outside. Mould Du-kit over outside wire to form beak.

POSITION OF CORD HOLES

4 cm from tip of head on top
3 cm from beak underneath
Diameter of hole approx 3 mm

BODY

Circumference at fattest point 9.5 cm.

LEGS

2 legs each of four twisted stiff wires 5 cm long
1.5 cm inside bird
3.5 cm outside bird with 1 cm of separated wires at end - bend three forward and one back to form feet

POSITION OF LEGS

7 cm from back of legs to tip of tail.
1 cm gap between but splay out a little so that the bird stands firmly.

THIMBLE

Press thimble in soft Du-kit to form a slight dip. This helps to prevent the pocket from sitting up too high.

fig. 2.

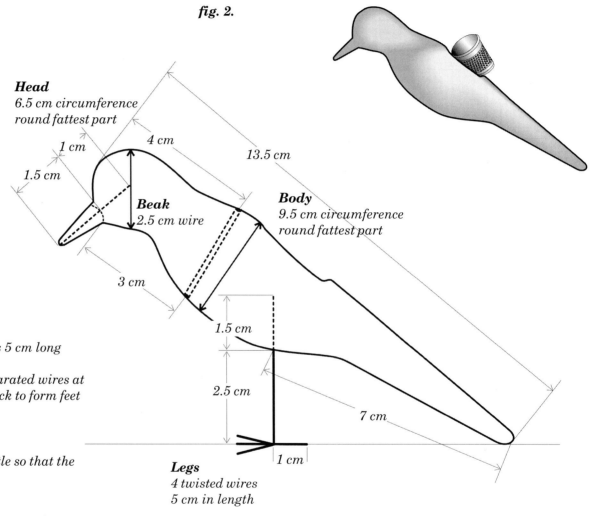

Head
6.5 cm circumference round fattest part

1 cm

1.5 cm

4 cm

13.5 cm

Beak
2.5 cm wire

Body
9.5 cm circumference round fattest part

3 cm

1.5 cm

2.5 cm

7 cm

Legs
4 twisted wires
5 cm in length

1 cm

LEGS

Make the legs from 2 x 5 cm lengths of four strand, twisted stiff wire (I used old washing line wire as it is *very* firm and stands well). With a 1 cm gap between the legs, push them into the body for 1.5 cms, leaving 3.5 cms of 'leg' exposed. At the end of each leg, untwist the four wires for 1 cm to create a foot, bending one wire backward and three forward.

BEAK

Using a single strand of the wire and cut off 2.5 cm for the beak. Push 1 cm into the head leaving 1.5 cm outside. Take the scrap of Du-kit and mould over the wire and onto the head to form a more rounded beak shape.

THIMBLE INDENTATION

Approximately 1.5 cm - (no more) down from the hole you made for the cord, press the thimble to form a slight indentation on the bird's back so that the thimble does not sit up too high and the pocket is less bulky. The larger, *open end* of the thimble should face the head end of the bird so that your finger can slip inside when the thimble is removed from the pocket.

TILTING THE HEAD

Just prior to 'baking' my bird I tilted the head to one side just a little. This makes him appear to be looking at you, which is rather nice, but entirely optional!

Bake in the oven as per the directions on the Du-kit packet

When cooled, ensure that the wires inserted into the bird stay firmly in place by putting a dab of UHU glue around the wire at the top of the legs in the little 'gap' between the wire and the clay.

COVERING THE BODY
LEGS AND BEAK

Using DM 273 Antique Gold thread and winding directly from the reel, place the end of the thread along a toe then wind the thread around the wire and the thread to cover the toe then whip down the next toe and back up to the next toe and so on covering each toe before covering the leg. Finish the thread at the top firmly by tying a slip knot, pull that tight and then make another 'clove hitch' knot. Leave a short end which is glued to the body, (or the head in the case of the beak), this will subsequently be covered by stitching. Wind the thread around the beak in the same way. (A light dab of glue stick at the tips of the toes and beak, will hold threads and prevent them falling off the ends.

BODY

The body is covered in a 'net' worked using fawn Perle No. 5 thread and a Tapestry No. 24 needle. It is important not to make the tension too tight as the embroidery needle and thread have to pass under the 'net' comfortably in subsequent stitching. However the net must be firm so that it can support all the feathers later sewn to it without sagging.

To start the net take the fawn thread and wind it one and a half times round the bird's neck anchoring the thread with a buttonhole stitch (fig. 3). Continue working buttonhole stitch round the bird's neck catching in the thread as you work (fig.4). Work buttonhole stitch round and round, working into the row above, increasing and decreasing as required to form a net all over the body (fig. 5).

The net goes completely over the bird's body, including the hollow for the thimble and needs to be loose enough to be depressed into the hollow when the thimble is in the pocket. The 'net' stretches over the shape, if the size of the net 'hole' in the

FOUNDATION STITCH OVER 'DU-KIT' BODY

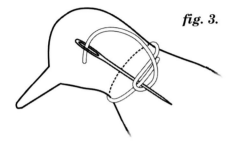

fig. 3.

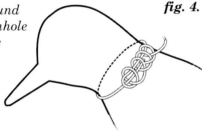

fig. 4.

Wrap thread clockwise round neck and then work buttonhole stitch in an anti-clockwise direction catching in the thread end as you work.

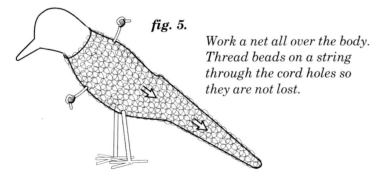

fig. 5.

Work a net all over the body. Thread beads on a string through the cord holes so they are not lost.

row above is looking a little wide add a stitch. If it is too narrow leave a stitch out. It is important to increase and decrease the stitches to keep the tension of the net right - not too tight and not too loose! Increase by working an extra buttonhole stitch or two and decrease by leaving one out.

To avoid 'losing' the cord holes in the bird's body when working the net, tie a bead onto one end of a thread then take it through the neck hole and tie a bead on the other end also, this is easily removed when you have finished the stitching but will make sure you don't lose the holes! Stitch round the legs, right down to the tail and then finish off your thread. To finish off the thread work back stitches into the net then take the end of the thread a short distance through the net.

Return to the beginning row of stitches at the neck and work, still in buttonhole stitch in the opposite direction, (fig. 6). Working from the neck, round the beak to the top of the head. Stitch round and round until you are nearing completion when you will find you have a small hole, close the small hole left by pulling the two sides of the gap together with an extra stitch or two (figs. 7 & 8).

EMBROIDERY OVER THE FOUNDATION NET

With the buttonhole 'net' now completely covering the bird it is time to work long and short stitch over the net to create a feathered appearance. In earlier birds made in this way the embroiderers did not work long and short stitch over the buttonhole stitch and the buttonhole stitches were worked more closely together but I chose to give my bird a more realistic appearance.

The long and short stitch is worked all over the body in colours resembling a kingfisher and the stitches are worked in the direction that the feathers would normally lie to give the texture and look of feathers. Use a Crewel No. 9 needle and two strands of rayon thread throughout (with the only exception being the very dark olive green stranded cotton where three threads are used), follow the colour chart for the bird in fig. 9.

Arrows have been marked on the kingfisher to give an indication of the direction for your stitching on the different areas of the bird's body. Remember that you are wishing to create the effect of feathers and work to cover the entire net foundation. The top of the back where the pocket will be need not be stitched to save unnecessary effort.

To secure your thread when starting and finishing, work a couple of little back stitches into the net, these will blend in with subsequent stitching

FEATHERS, TAIL AND BODY, AND THE POCKET

The final stage in the decoration of the kingfisher is made up of three steps: stitching and applying the tail feathers, the construction of the thimble pocket and finally stitching and applying the body feathers. At all times remember that your bird will be slightly different from ours - and remember to allow for this.

FEATHERS

The kingfisher is covered in a beautiful array of finely coloured feathers. These feathers are not hard to make but will take time! They are made in an embroidery hoop on a firm base, except for the final ones stitched directly to the body. The feathers are worked in picot stitch with the long tail feathers worked in extended picot stitch using four strands of DMC and Marlitt thread and a tapestry needle No. 24. When the feathers are worked directly onto the bird a crewel No. 9 needle is better as it can easily go through all the underneath materials. This is creative sewing, be flexible! For full instructions on working picot stitch please refer to page 13.

fig. 6.

Return to cast on line and work back towards the head

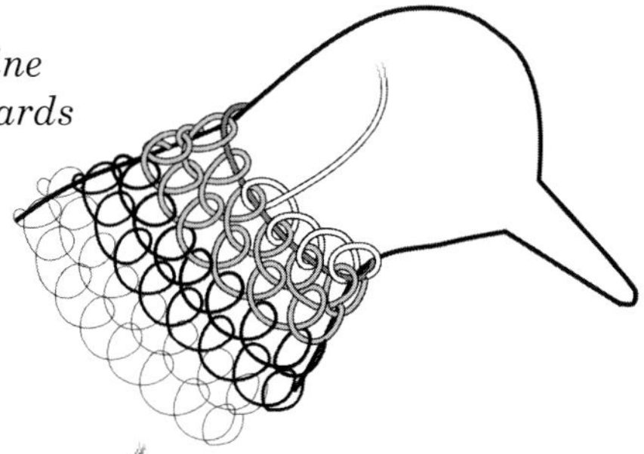

fig. 7.

Cover head allowing the beak to protrude through the 'net'

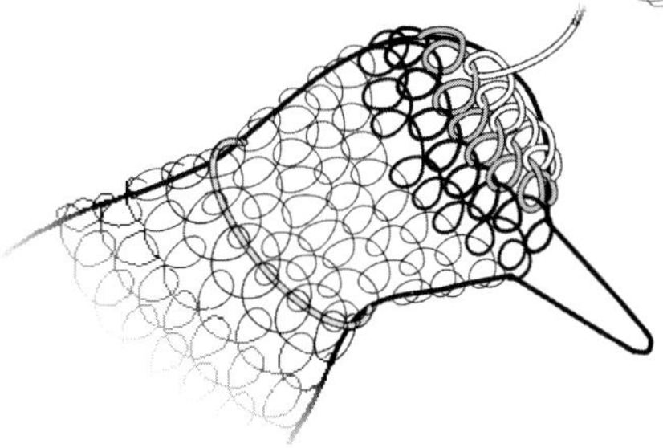

fig. 8.

To finish off at the top of the head work round and round until left with a small 'hole', make last row joining into the row opposite to close the hole

97

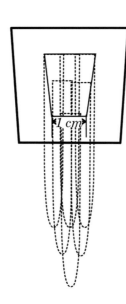

fig. 10.

OUTLINE FOR BASE
dotted line shows area feathers worked in, stitch feathers on base then attach to bird

finished width 1-1.5 cm at top end and 1 cm at lower end

For best results it is important to stitch the following steps in the sequence given.

TAIL FEATHERS

The pattern for the base is given in fig. 10. Draw the outline of the base onto your material (do not cut out), then place the material into your frame and secure firmly. The feathers are worked in the area outlined with a dotted line.

Make about seven long tail feathers, working them in rows directly onto the base material. The feathers are about 8 to 10 mm wide at the top and are about 5 cms long and have been made in the following colours, two dark Pacific turquoise, one Pacific turquoise, two lagoon green, one dark glacier turquoise and one glacier turquoise.

Begin with the bottom layer and then work up the shape overlapping the feathers as you go. When you have made the required number of feathers, cut out the base shape, turn under the edges and slip stitch the base with feathers worked on it, to the body end of the tail making sure that it is positioned on the top of the tail. The tail feathers should extend 1 - 1.5 cm beyond the 'solid' tail - refer to fig. 11 for placement.

Your tail may still appear a little bare and our bird does have an additional four feathers worked directly onto his body. But it is better if the last tail feathers are worked when the bird has his body feathers sewn on too as then you have more idea where best to place them. The feathers worked directly onto the bird are positioned to fill in gaps, hide ribbon endings and generally to perfect the appearance of the bird. Instructions for working these final tail feathers are given near the end of the instructions.

THE POCKET LINING

The pocket on the back of the kingfisher is designed to hold a thimble. It is important when making the pocket for your thimble to take into account that your bird's body and also your thimble may very well be different to the one illustrated. The pattern given allows plenty of material to be turned in, so trim as necessary. Check as you go that the pocket fits over your thimble comfortably. Be prepared to make adjustments as you assemble the pocket to allow for variations in the size of the thimble and the size of the bird.

Trace a pocket lining pattern, a seam allowance is included, then using your pattern cut the lining out of fine, matching coloured material. Pin the *small end* of the lining (called 'base of pocket'), right side up onto the bird, turn under the 'head edge' and slip stitch into position just below the cord hole see fig 11. Stitch across the top first to get the placement correct. Then stitch down each side to the 'fold forward line'.

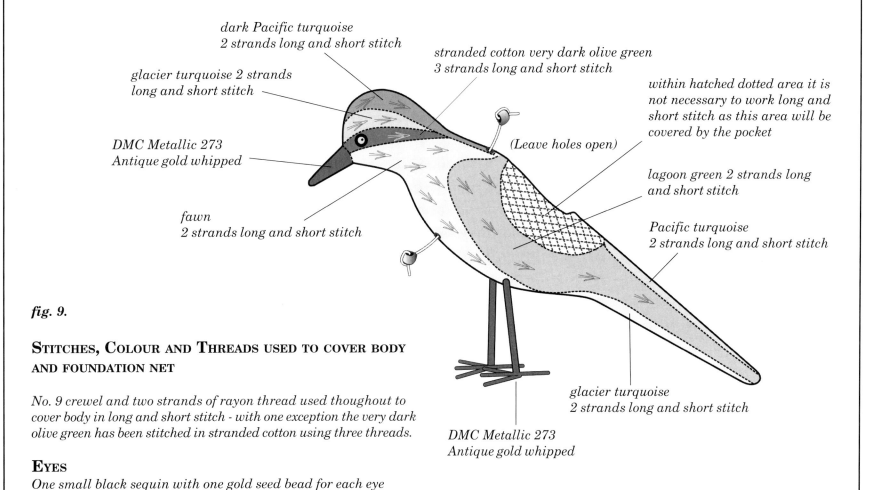

dark Pacific turquoise
2 strands long and short stitch

glacier turquoise 2 strands
long and short stitch

stranded cotton very dark olive green
3 strands long and short stitch

within hatched dotted area it is
not necessary to work long and
short stitch as this area will be
covered by the pocket

DMC Metallic 273
Antique gold whipped

(Leave holes open)

lagoon green 2 strands long
and short stitch

fawn
2 strands long and short stitch

Pacific turquoise
2 strands long and short stitch

glacier turquoise
2 strands long and short stitch

DMC Metallic 273
Antique gold whipped

fig. 9.

STITCHES, COLOUR AND THREADS USED TO COVER BODY AND FOUNDATION NET

No. 9 crewel and two strands of rayon thread used thoughout to cover body in long and short stitch - with one exception the very dark olive green has been stitched in stranded cotton using three threads.

EYES
One small black sequin with one gold seed bead for each eye

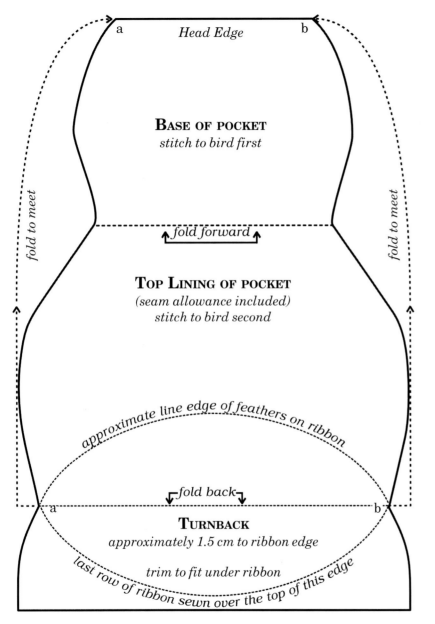

Head Edge

a   b

BASE OF POCKET
stitch to bird first

fold to meet   fold to meet

↑ *fold forward* ↑

TOP LINING OF POCKET
(seam allowance included)
stitch to bird second

approximate line edge of feathers on ribbon

⌐*fold back*⌐

a   b

TURNBACK
approximately 1.5 cm to ribbon edge

trim to fit under ribbon

last row of ribbon sewn over the top of this edge

Fold forward the large 'top lining of the pocket' taking 'a' to 'a' and 'b' to 'b' - the centre of this folded edge extends about 6 mm beyond the already attached base of the pocket at the centre top, but only overlaps the base of the pocket slightly at the sides (fig. 11).

The top section sits up higher to allow easy access to your thimble, but when pulled tight with the cord, it sits, just covering the lining *directly below the cord hole*. Pin the sides down then check the opening is big enough for the thimble and your finger to fit into, adjust as required. Trim if needed, turn under edges and slip stitch down over the top of the 'base of pocket', easing in fullness along the side. Do not slip stitch the 'turn back' down at this stage. The pattern allows for wide variation in thimble size, you may need to trim back the fabric quite extensively.

At this point you need to cut out the pocket top and attach it to the bird.

THE POCKET TOP

Trace the pattern for the pocket top, seam allowances included, and use this pattern to cut out the pocket top from your fabric (fine strong fabric but will not be seen). Now position the pocket top (which goes over the thimble and the top lining of the pocket and creates the bird's back) so that the feathers at the lower end will just overlap the tail feathers. With the thimble in the pocket make any adjustments required then turn under the raw edges and slip stitch the pocket top across the bottom and over the side edges of the lining. The pocket top is left separate from the pocket lining at the top as it is easier to stitch the ribbon to the pocket top without catching the pocket lining if you can slip your fingers inside to separate the two layers of material. The body feathers are worked onto ribbon, one row at a time and stitched to the pocket top working from the base of the pocket up.

POCKET TOP
base for feathers
(seam allowance included)
stitch to bird third

BODY FEATHERS

The body feathers, like the tail feathers, are worked in picot stitch. They are all very similar in size but much shorter than the tail feathers varying between 1 - 1.5 cm in length and between 8 - 10 mm in width at the top. They are worked in rows on fine, lightweight ribbon which has been pinned to a vylene base held firmly in an embroidery hoop. When the rows of feathers are completed they are slip stitched to the pocket top. The number of feathers in each row varies as the pocket shape increases - some rows had eight feathers some eleven with extras added after the pocket top had been sewn on, to cover the ends.

A selection from seven different colours has been used to create the shading in the body feathers of the kingfisher, each side is balanced to match the other. To keep the balance of colour I worked one and sometimes two of each shade up to the centre then I would work the feathers correspondingly on the other side, for example 0-1-2-3-4-5-4-3-2-1-0. All these colours go together well so stitch the feathers in any arrangement that you like (fig.12).

TO WORK THE FEATHERS ONTO NARROW RIBBON

Choose very light weight ribbon, rayon, silk or nylon in preference to satin. If possible choose ribbon exactly the same colour as your fabric or one that tones well as the ribbon is seen in the top row.

Cover a small frame with medium weight vylene. Lay your ribbon over the top of the pocket (with the thimble inside) to find the length of ribbon required for the row of feathers, add a little extra for a turn under at each end, then pin the ribbon to the vylene on the frame. The feathers are worked in the *centre* of the ribbon, (except for the very last row of feathers) right up to the point where the ribbon will be turned under (fig. 12).

Work as many feathers in picot stitch as are needed to fill the length of each row. Remove the ribbon from the vylene, trim the vylene back to the stitches so that no vylene shows at all. The beauty of vylene is that you can cut out one row of feathers, leaving holes in the vylene but then re-use it for working the next row of feathers.

Slip stitch the rows of feathers onto the top pocket. Begin at the tail end and work up to the pocket opening. Remember to alternate the completed rows of feathers on the pocket top (kingfisher's back), so that the feathers overlap the feathers in the row below (fig. 13). When you are stitching the feathers to the

fig. 11.

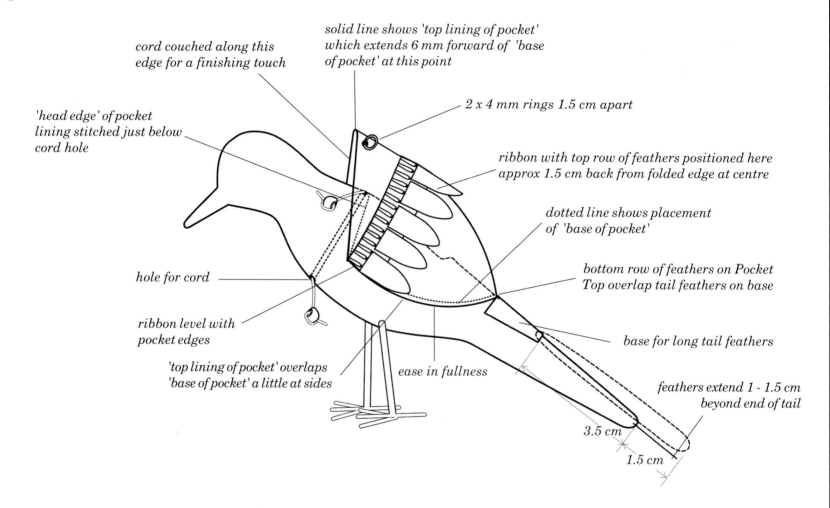

cord couched along this
edge for a finishing touch

solid line shows 'top lining of pocket'
which extends 6 mm forward of 'base
of pocket' at this point

'head edge' of pocket
lining stitched just below
cord hole

2 x 4 mm rings 1.5 cm apart

ribbon with top row of feathers positioned here
approx 1.5 cm back from folded edge at centre

dotted line shows placement
of 'base of pocket'

hole for cord

bottom row of feathers on Pocket
Top overlap tail feathers on base

ribbon level with
pocket edges

base for long tail feathers

'top lining of pocket' overlaps
'base of pocket' a little at sides

ease in fullness

feathers extend 1 - 1.5 cm
beyond end of tail

3.5 cm

1.5 cm

pocket top slip your fingers between the lining and the pocket top so that the stitches do not catch the lining.

The top row of feathers are worked on the *very bottom edge* of the ribbon and are positioned about 1.5 cm away from the top edge of the thimble pocket in the centre but level with the pocket at each side (fig. 11).

To neaten the top edge, the 'pocket top' can be slipped under the 'turn back' of the pocket lining. Then fold the 'turn back' of the pocket lining down and trim so that it fits neatly beneath the last row of ribbon. If your material is inclined to fray it could be a good idea to turn under the raw edge of the pocket lining, then sew the top edge of the ribbon over the top of the neatened pocket lining and all the raw edges have been dealt with!

To soften the ribbon edge detached chain stitch has been worked over the ribbon using one thread of a toning colour (fig. 14).

EXTRA FEATHERS

To fill in and cover the ribbon ends at the end of each row, the edges where the pocket joins the bird and any other gaps near the tail, extra feathers are stitched directly on to the bird in the appropriate places. These also improve the balance and appearance of the kingfisher.

These need to be worked directly on the bird, so care must be taken not to snag your embroidery thread on previously made feathers when the pin is inserted. The feathers in the row above where you intend to begin to stitch will also have to be lifted out of the way when you are starting and whilst stitching. Work from the tail to the head as the feathers overlap nicely this way.

I worked a further four tail feathers. Two worked in dark Pacific turquoise are placed to each side of the central group and two more worked in glacier turquoise are placed right down on the lower edge of the 'solid' tail.

fig. 12.

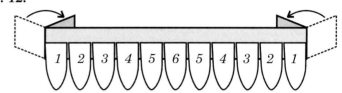

feathers worked down the centre of 10 mm ribbon and stitched right up to the turned under edge of ribbon at each end

fig. 13.

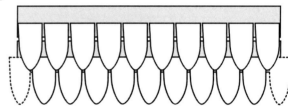

place feathers alternately in rows to overlap the row below extra feathers can be added at the side

fig. 14.

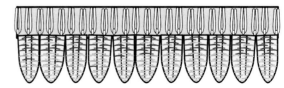

fig. 15.

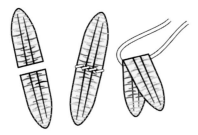

four small feathers worked directly onto vylene
trim away vylene and stitch together at widest part, fold, slip over
cord then stitch together

I also worked an extra four feathers on each side of the body. These were worked in colours to match the existing edge feathers and were positioned to cover the lining, ribbon ends and one slightly longer (2.5 cm) which sweeps back from the body towards the tail helping to make the feathers from the body 'flow' into the tail feathers.

FINISHING OFF

The pocket edge is then decorated by couching on a piece of 1 mm cord if desired. (I used the same cord here as I subsequently used for the little drawstring which tightens the thimble pocket.) The beginning and ending of the cord is hidden under the side feathers.

Stitch 2 x 4 mm rings 1.5 cm apart at the centre of the top of the pocket. Thread a 1 mm cord through the two little rings on the pocket then take both ends down through the hole in its chest and knot.

Attach a little picot feather at each end of the doubled cord, one picot feather will hide the knot joining the cord together. To make these two feathers, work directly onto vylene in a small frame. The four small feathers are worked back to back. Trim away the vylene backing, stitch together at the widest part with sewing cotton then fold in half and slip over the cord and stitch together round the edge (fig. 15).

This cord enables you to close the pocket by pulling the picot feather on the birds chest, keeping your thimble safely inside the little pocket. To open the pocket to get your thimble out pull the picot feather on the pocket.

Sew on one black sequin and one gold seed bead for each eye and your very special kingfisher thimble holder is complete.

You have created an 'heirloom' of the future, treasure it.